STOP
HURTING
START
HEALING

GASPAR & MICHELE ANASTASI

WORD OF LIFE PRESS

2150 COLLIER AVE., SUITE H, FORT MYERS, FLORIDA 33901
www.WOLM.net

ISBN 193204837-5

Unless otherwise specified all Bible references are from
the King James version.

CONTENTS

INTRODUCTION

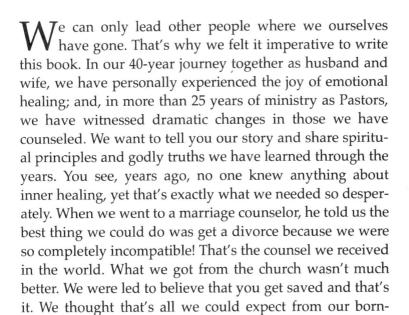

W e can only lead other people where we ourselves have gone. That's why we felt it imperative to write this book. In our 40-year journey together as husband and wife, we have personally experienced the joy of emotional healing; and, in more than 25 years of ministry as Pastors, we have witnessed dramatic changes in those we have counseled. We want to tell you our story and share spiritual principles and godly truths we have learned through the years. You see, years ago, no one knew anything about inner healing, yet that's exactly what we needed so desperately. When we went to a marriage counselor, he told us the best thing we could do was get a divorce because we were so completely incompatible! That's the counsel we received in the world. What we got from the church wasn't much better. We were led to believe that you get saved and that's it. We thought that's all we could expect from our born-again experience. *But God....*

It has been a long journey, but God has led us so graciously and taught us so many things, and we know the principles we share with you in this book work because they are what God used to heal us. And what healing He has done in our lives! Individually and as a couple, we have been rescued from the deepest depths of defeat, depravity and depression and raised to the very throne room of God where He gave us victory, respect and wholeness in our marriage and our lives! Nothing this world offered us could have accomplished that.

Take a moment and look at the cover of this book. We believe that our journey in life is similar to the journey of this leaf. We go through seasons of great hope and expectation and also seasons of crisis and seeming defeat. We are often swept away by the issues of life, battered by the wind, crushed on the rocks and left hurt and deeply wounded. All of us have some degree of emotional damage. It's impossible to brave the journey of life without getting injured. We want to help you stop the hurt and start the process of healing. In this book, God is pouring out a river of living water to heal your body, soul, spirit and relationships. Come and drink!

It is our prayer and firm belief that the truths we share will free you from past hurts and heal your damaged emotions.

CHAPTER ONE
OUR JOURNEY BEGINS

B ack in the early 70's, we were a young married couple and we were really struggling—struggling to find answers to life and trying everything that the world offered us, only to find that this search just made us more thirsty, hungry and desperate than ever before. Sound familiar? Can you put yourself in this scenario?

Because of the pain I (Gaspar) felt deep inside, I went on a journey alone, leaving everything and everyone that was near and dear to me. I was desperate, feeling isolated and, perhaps like you, looking for answers to my life. The farther I wandered the worse I got, and I found myself in even deeper trouble. Finally I concluded I had no reason left to live. Every decision I had made up to that point had been wrong and had only heaped more and more condemnation and self-rejection upon me. I thought the best thing to do was to kill myself. (It is amazing how far down the road of depression a person can travel without God. But, no matter how far we wander from Him, He never leaves us or forsakes us.) What I went through during that long dark season of my life was all part of His plan. He knew I had to come to the end of myself before I could find Him—not that

He was lost. He was there all the time. I just wasn't looking for Him... until I got desperate.

Little did I know but, at that time, my wife Michele had given her heart to the Lord. She turned full control of her life over to God, allowing His Word to guide her every step. An incredible change took place in her and she began to pray for me. She was really gracious to pray for me, considering the lifestyle I led at that time. She had become a completely different person. Thank God for His grace!

I was too consumed with my problems and my self to realize she was praying for me. Then the Lord began speaking to my heart. He showed me His great love and a way out of my bondage. He revealed His Son Jesus to me. What an eye-opening, heart-changing experience! When I accepted Him, I was alone in the country feeling suicidal. I just broke down weeping before the Lord. It was as though a black cloud lifted off me. He intervened that day and brought deliverance, healing and salvation to my life. I was instantly changed! I truly felt like I was born all over again.

I had always talked about Jesus, heard the priests talk about Him, read books about Him, but I didn't know Him personally. I was in absolute awe! I was instantaneously brought into a love relationship with the Lover of my soul. That day He miraculously changed the many things I wanted to change and couldn't. Just a few minutes in His presence altered my destiny forever. I began a new journey in life that gets more exciting and joyful every day.

THE REAL WORK STARTS

It took desperation to come to the end of self and finally allow God to do what He always wanted to do in my life. But I thought that was the end of the journey. I didn't realize how much God needed to do in me so that my life could be used for His glory. Salvation began that day, but it was only the beginning of changes that would take the rest of my life to complete. God wanted me saved, but He also wanted to heal me from the inside out. He wanted to do things in me that no one else could. That's why He is called the Great Physician. His hands can go where no knife can.

After I met God in the country that day, I came to understand something about Him that wasn't widely known in the 70's. Everybody understood that God is love. What I learned was that He cared about me—the whole person. I knew He loved me in a general way, but I found out He was actually interested in my feelings and my emotions. **He cared about the hurts I carried in my mind as well as my body.** He was interested in healing all of me. What revelation this was!

After that, I attended church and accepted the Lord all over again. I told the Pastor that, even though I had had a wonderful experience with God, I must have missed something because I was still hurting on the inside. I had a smile on my face, but I was filled with pain. He said, "Maybe you need to get saved all over again." The Pastor meant well, but he had no understanding of the concept of spirit, soul and body. He had never heard of inner healing. Churches believed in healing, but it was restricted to physical healing. There was little or no understanding of inner healing.

I knew something was very wrong. Everyone else seemed so happy to me, going their merry way. However, I was dealing with rejection; I was wounded and I felt broken inside. It seemed like there was no one I could talk to about the pain I was feeling. I wanted to scream, "I might look good, but I am suffering and dying on the inside!" (As a

Pastor, I now know that many people carry that stifled cry inside.)

So I went back to my Pastor. He said, "Well, maybe you don't have enough faith." He figured that I must be saved since he had seen me go up to the altar ten times! So, to him, the only logical problem had to be lack of faith. I thought to myself, "What does that mean—more faith?" I devoured the Word of God, trying to get more faith so I could believe that I was really saved. Then, thank God, He showed me in His Word that He not only saved my spirit, but He wanted to walk me through this journey and save my soul (my mind, will and emotions)!

My soul was broken, wounded and severely bruised because, my whole life, I had made decisions which brought me much pain and hurt. I had a born again spirit and I knew I was on my way to heaven, but I was dealing with major issues. To put it bluntly, I was dysfunctional! I was like many Christians today. The problem is that we are "soulish" or carnal Christians and we really haven't been saved in our souls. We are hurting and wounded and, as you know, hurt people hurt people. That is why so many churches are splitting and so many families are falling apart. That's why so many Christians change friends and relationships like they change clothes. They are hurt and emotionally crippled.

During that period of rapid spiritual growth, God began to show me how much He loved and cared for me. He was not just concerned about getting me to heaven. **He wanted me to live every day of my life in the glory of His presence and with His healing power in my life.** So He began to separate me from doctrines and denominations and teach me the truth about healing.

MICHELE'S JOURNEY

I (Michele) was the poster child for bitterness. The sad part was that I did not even know I was bitter. Everyone else knew it, but I was the last to know. I thought that bitter people were like the old lady down the block who yelled at the kids and looked like she sucked on lemons, but not me. I wasn't bitter.

Actually my testimony goes back even further, back to childhood. I was raised in an abusive home. My mom was physically and emotionally abusive, but she called it discipline. She didn't know any better because that's how she was raised. When you discipline a child harshly and withhold love from her, it breeds anger, rebellion and bitterness. That's what happened to me. I thought that when I got married, I would leave the bitterness behind and start a new life, **but bitterness is like a poison. You can't leave it behind; it is inside you and goes wherever you go.** Because I was never given forgiveness, I did not know how to forgive. To my mom, I was "the bad daughter". I will never forget how my mother presented me to my mother-in-law the first time they met. She pointed to me and said, "This is my bad daughter… and this is my good daughter," pointing to my sister. Nice impression on my future mother-in-law, right?

My mother kept a list of things I did wrong. When I got married and my husband did something to hurt me (as all mates do), I just swallowed a little bit more bitterness each time. Instead of keeping a list like my mother, I kept a journal. I had it all right there—all the poison. The thing about this poison is that it does not stay in one little part of your life. It ends up consuming all relationships and, in our case, it actually brought us to the brink of divorce.

A MINISTRY IS BORN

Now here we were together on this journey as a couple in the church. We were what you would call the "walking wounded", but thank God the Holy Spirit was teaching us. We began to realize that there was more to us than meets the eye. When we started dealing with our "soulish" issues, even though we were born again, things did not suddenly get fixed. They got worse. That is a key point to understand. **Becoming Christian does not mean everything is going to get better right away.** Yes, you are on your way to heaven and will escape hell, but coming face to face with God really shows you how much work needs to be done in your life.

We strayed from the thinking of contemporary preachers who said, "You are born again now and everything is passed away." II Corinthians 5:17 does say "therefore if any man be in Christ, he's a new creature, old things are passed away, behold all things are become new." We believe that the "new creature" or new creation refers to our born again spirit, but not to every facet of our lives. We knew our spirits were born again, but there were a lot a things in our lives that still needed to be fixed.

However, we kept going and, eventually we were raised up to pastor a church. Not only did God raise us up as pastors, but He graciously gave us a huge building that seated over two thousand people. (This was over 25 years ago. We only had about fifteen members at the time, and five of them were our own family!)

As we went through these changes in our own lives, we soon realized that God was placing an anointing and a mantle on us for inner healing. At the same time we ourselves were being healed, He was teaching us how to minister what we learned to others. From that, He birthed the prayer counseling ministry and gave us an anointing to restore broken marriages through marriage conferences, marriage workshops and retreats. For at least 20 years now, we have been conducting "Damaged Emotions and Past Hurts" conferences once or twice a year. Our ministry doesn't come from something we read in a book. It comes from first-hand experience.

The godly principles we learned along our journey even laid the foundation for our New Life Centers for men and women, a residential restoration program for drug and alcohol abusers. It has been in existence for more than twenty years.

We wrote this book because we have personally seen and experienced the principles we're about to share with you radically transform lives, starting with ours. We know God is a God of inner healing. **Our heavenly Father wants to heal the WHOLE PERSON! He wants to heal YOU.**

CHAPTER TWO
THE PROCESS OF SALVATION

You may be searching for answers like we were in those early years of our marriage, or maybe you've already come to the end of yourself and given your life to Jesus. Someone preached the Gospel to you, which is a blessing, but they may have also promised you a trouble-free life, and now you're a little confused because that hasn't been your experience. I have heard many preachers say, "Give your life to Jesus and all your problems will be gone." To some extent that is true: Our biggest problem is gone—eternal death. The Bible says that the wages of sin is death, and Jesus Christ paid the price for all our sins. We are all saved by God's grace and we have eternal life through His sacrifice. But the Bible also tells us in many places that there will be trials. "Many are the afflictions of the righteous but the Lord delivereth him out of them all" (Psalm 34:19).

So here we are, baby Christians saved by grace, thrilled that all our problems are over and BOOM! We get blown completely out of the water by problems. That's why so many believers get confused and discouraged. We're saved, but instead of getting better, suddenly everything gets worse. What on earth is going on?

A WORK IN PROGRESS

God is working on us, and He often uses the trials we face to perfect us. There are still things in our heart that God wants to deal with or get rid of altogether and He uses our difficulties to do it. He is restoring our soul and our relationships. He is healing us from the inside out: the feelings, thoughts, bad memories and other baggage from the past that we try to carry into our Christian life. It's impossible to go through life and not bear *some* scars, unhealed wounds or painful memories. Those are the things God wants to work on.

There are negative thought patterns that are deeply ingrained in your mind because of things you experienced in the past and you don't even realize it. Think about it. When you accepted Jesus Christ, did everything negative leave your life? Sure, some things did change, but I am sure there must be others that have not changed and remain even to this day. Although you may be a Christian ten, fifteen or twenty years, there are still some issues left to deal with.

Then while God is working out His plans in your life, the devil jumps on the bandwagon, telling you that you are a loser, you are not saved; you don't have it right and God loves other people more than you. What a lie! Satan is the father of all lies. Remember that he is also called the accuser of the brethren. If you are a "brethren", a member of the household of faith through Jesus Christ, he will accuse you.

Please understand that God is working on the inside of you. You are under construction. Praise the Lord! **He accepts you just the way you are, but He loves you enough not to let you stay that way!** We are His special project! "Except the Lord build the house, they labor in vain that build it..." (Psalm 127:1). God wants to bulldoze that

STOP HURTING START HEALING

little shanty you've been building for yourself your whole life, so He can build you a mansion.

To use another analogy, we are like clay in the Potter's hand and, since we now belong to Him, He is determined to mold us into the vessels that He wants us to be. God told the prophet Jeremiah:

> Arise and go down to the potter's house, and there I will cause you to hear My words." Then I went down to the potter's house and there he was, making something at the wheel. And the vessel that he made of clay was marred in the hand of the potter; so he made it into another vessel, as it seemed good to the potter to make. Then the word of the Lord came to me saying: "O house of Israel, can I not do with you as this potter?" says the Lord. "Look, as the clay is in the potter's hand, so are you in My hand, O house of Israel! (Jeremiah 18:2-4)

Many times we resist God when He is tearing down the old, when He is re-molding and re-shaping us into something new. We fight to hold on to our old ways because they are comfortable to us, but God cannot put new wine in old wineskins. He has to make us new. Of course, we all want His new wine, the best wine, the wine He has been saving for these end times in which we now live! Our job is to be willing vessels that He can pour Himself into and use for His purposes. We touched on II Corinthians 5:17 in the introduction, but let's take another look at it:

> Therefore if any man be in Christ, he is a new creature, old things are passed away, behold all things are become new. (II Cor. 5:17)

People still believe that when we accept Jesus Christ as Lord and Savior, we've received as much as we're going to get from God. We've got our ticket to heaven and all we have to do is get through life the best way we can until the trumpet sounds. They think: *If I try real hard to just grin and bear it, if I can hang in there until He takes me home to glory, I'll*

17

be okay. Yet, in the Church, you and I are still dealing with major issues. We walk in bitterness, rejection, criticism and discord. **What's the point of being born again only to live a defeated life? No, Church, God has a better plan.**

CHANGED: SPIRIT, SOUL AND BODY

Salvation is a process that starts on the day you give your heart to the Lord. Your spirit is saved immediately, but the salvation of your soul (your thoughts, feelings, rationale, logic and memory) is a process God completes over time.

> *Therefore, if any man be in Christ, he is a new creature; old things are passed away; behold, all things are become new. And all things are of God... (II Cor. 5:17, 18)*

Another translation calls us a "new species of being". He is talking about your spirit. There is more to you than meets the eye. You are a spirit; you have a soul; and you live in a body. If a person could look beyond your physical body through the windows of your eyes, they would see your soul and spirit. That is the real you. Your soul and spirit are what make you who you are. It does not matter what color the house is, it is who lives on the inside that counts. Amen?

When you accepted Jesus as Lord and Savior, He immediately transformed your spirit into a new species of being, but what about the other two aspects of your being: your body and your soul? When you become born again, when your spirit is brand new and has the very nature of Christ, you now have a solid foundation God can begin to build on and bring healing to the rest of you. Your born again spirit is the sound foundation He needs to start His work. **After your spirit is renewed, He goes to work on your soul.** When you really get hold of the revelation that God wants to heal the whole person from the inside out, that's when you'll start to see real growth in your life. You'll stop resisting the Great Physician and let Him go into the deep places of your life where no knife can go, cutting out some things and mending others, as only He can. You'll yield to the process necessary for Him and change your life. It's time to get out of dysfunction and become functional Christians, a Body Jesus can truly use.

IT'S ALL ABOUT FORGIVENESS

If I could use just one word to describe the born again experience, I would say "forgiven". The new birth and forgiveness are linked; they are one and the same. The first thing that happens when you receive God's forgiveness is the new birth. The power of God's forgiveness causes your spirit to be regenerated and made new.

Jesus said He came to give us life and life more abundantly (John10:10). Of course we are living, but He came to give us a life that's more excellent, more fulfilled, more rewarding than anything we've ever experienced—the *zoë*, absolute, eternal, everlasting life of God. God wants to give us *His* life. How does He do that? By forgiving our sins and reconciling (restoring) us to Himself. Jesus made the way for our forgiveness and abundant life by laying down His life and taking our punishment on the cross.

Forgiveness is the central theme of the whole Bible. From the beginning of Genesis to the end of Revelation, God is reaching out to man, letting us know that forgiveness is available to us through the shed blood of Jesus Christ, so we can be restored to an intimate, personal relationship with Him.

And all things are of God, who hath reconciled us to Himself by Jesus Christ, and hath given us the ministry of reconciliation. (II Cor. 5:18)

God has reconciled or restored our relationship with Himself through Jesus Christ. The word "reconcile" in the dictionary means: a.) to restore to harmony; b). to bring to resolution. How wonderful it is that our God wants to restore us to harmony with Himself and to resolve our sin problem! How wonderful it is that He puts His arms around us, loves us, cares for us—is intimate and personal with us!

Wow! He is God. Do you realize how big God is? Do you understand how powerful and awesome He is? He created everything that ever existed and ever will exist. Isn't it amazing that this same God yearns to be in relationship with you and has done the greatest thing He could ever do for you by coming down from heaven and dying on the cross of Calvary so that you could be one with Him? And it's all about forgiveness. Amazing, isn't it?

Think about this for a moment. **No other religion preaches forgiveness of sins for all mankind. No other religion worships a God that sacrificed Himself to show His love for mankind. Yet, in churches today, forgiveness is barely mentioned.** What a shame!

THE SACRIFICIAL SYSTEM

In Genesis, we see the holy bond of fellowship that Adam and Eve shared with God. They walked in the Garden of Eden with Him in the cool of the day. Imagine the conversations they must have shared with Him and the intimate love that they experienced with their Father. They were clothed in His glory. Then sin corrupted their heart and separated them from Him. How tragic! But even before Adam and Eve sinned, long before the foundation of the world in fact, God had a plan to extend to man His forgiveness. The first thing He did after Adam and Eve's fall was to shed the blood of an animal (Genesis 3:21). He did this for two reasons: to clothe their sinful flesh and to reconcile them to Himself. The Creator knew that sin created a gulf between Himself and His precious creation, yet He still wanted to be in relationship with them. The sacrifice of the animal was a shadow and type of things to come—our ultimate forgiveness and reconciliation through the shed blood of Jesus.

When God delivered Israel out of Egypt, He told them to take a three-day journey into the wilderness so they could worship Him. When they got to Mount Sinai, He revealed to them how He was to be worshiped. When God met with Moses, He gave instructions for the system of animal sacrifice we see used throughout the Old Testament. Holy God reached out to sinful man because there could be no relationship until the sin problem was dealt with. Divine forgiveness came through the atoning blood of the sacrifice.

Day and night, year round, smoke was curling up into the air as the priests offered up the sacrifices of Yahweh. Wherever the children of Israel went, they saw the smoke, which gave them peace in their hearts. They knew that God had covered their sins and they were one with Him. They understood that He had made a way to be their God, and that they were His people. They knew He accepted their sacrifices and they were forgiven. Throughout the Bible, God is drawing us into a whole relationship through divine forgiveness. He showed us that He was willing to pay the ultimate price to forgive us, because we could not do it ourselves. I believe that John 1:29 reveals the heart of God.

The next day, John seeth Jesus coming unto him, and sayeth, 'Behold, the lamb of God which taketh away the sins of the world.' (John 1:29)

John the Baptist was announcing that Jesus was the final sacrifice, once and for all. Goats, sheep and bulls no longer needed to be killed and burned on the altar. The burnt offerings, wave offerings and all the other various offerings could not fulfill the Law. Only Jesus could fulfill it because He alone was sinless and would willingly lay down His life which the animals had taken from them by force. On the cross He said, "It is finished." It is done. The price for our sins is paid in full! He is saying right now, "If you will just believe in Me, just walk in Me; if you will just accept what I have done, you will have instantaneous access to the heart of God. Just receive My forgiveness for all of your sins. You cannot earn it. Do not even try. **I will empower you to live a Christ-like life.**" Jesus did exactly what John the Baptist proclaimed that day at the river. His whole purpose in coming was to be the sacrificial Lamb of God and take away the sins of the world.

In Old Testament times, when the High Priest went into the Holy of Holies on Yom Kippur, the Day of Atonement, there were specific things he had to do to prepare himself. Before entering through the veil to stand before the mercy seat (the ark of the covenant) in the Holy of Holies, He had to take a ritual bath and follow other stringent rules to assure that He was "clean". He had to carry with him the blood of an animal to atone for his sins. Even with all the strict preparations, he had to make sure that smoke filled the Holy of Holies so that his flesh would not be visible. Nothing of the flesh can glory in the presence of God. Bells sewn to the hem of his robe jingled as he moved about behind the veil to let anyone outside the veil know he was still alive. He also tied a rope around his leg so that if, by chance, he was unclean and he died in the presence of God, the other priests could pull him out. What a scary scenario!

SELF: THE ULTIMATE SACRIFICE

You may be wondering what all of that means to us as Christians today. All that sacrificial stuff was Old Testament, right? But God still operates according to the same principles. He tells us that He changeth not. He is the same yesterday, today and forever (Hebrews 13:8). As royal priests, His chosen people, we are to come boldly to the throne of grace (Heb. 4:16). He also says that no flesh can stand in His presence. That's why, like the Old Testament priests, we come with the blood of the Lamb, Jesus Christ, clothed in the priestly garments of Jesus' righteousness, and we bring the sacrifice of our own flesh.

> *I beseech you therefore brethren, by the mercies of God, that ye present your bodies as a living sacrifice holy and acceptable unto God, which is your reasonable service. (Romans 12:1)*

God wants us to sacrifice ourselves on His altar but, too often, pride stands in the way. It is not about *me, mine* and *I*. Pride has to go. Notice that the letter "I" is smack in the middle of the word PRIDE! We have to get rid of *I*! "I" is also the first letter in the Hebrew word *Ichabod* which means the glory has departed. *Ichabod* is the opposite of *chabod*, the glory and presence of God. As you and I crucify the big "I" in our lives, that part of us that just wants its own way, we will truly see the *chabod*, the glory of God manifest in His Church.

I know that every believer wants to sense the glory of God in their life. The true Body of Christ hungers to have the presence of God in their midst during worship services. So, if the way to kill the glory of God is to keep "I" in the center of my life, then let's get rid of "I"! You can't have two kings sitting on the same throne. God is a gentleman and He won't force His way. He'll leave instead. Don't let Him!

Jesus tells us to take up our cross and follow Him. Taking His cross means crucifying ourselves daily, and that often means forgiving those who hurt us (Matt. 10:38). We've already established that forgiveness is the central theme of the salvation process. To forgive, we must crucify our flesh. There is no other way. When we, with the help of the Holy Spirit, crucify self and die to our own ways and our own feelings, God will release resurrection power in our lives!

When you extend forgiveness, you release from bondage the people that hurt you and you actually release healing to yourself. You hold the key that unlocks the door for the healing and salvation of the people who hurt you the most. God saved you, equipped you and then placed you in relationship with them so He can express His love for them through forgiveness. Stop waiting for him or her to make the first move. Bring your own flesh and willingly lay it on the altar so that God can be glorified.

BECOME BORN AGAIN

As we stated earlier, success in healing begins with the new birth into the family of God. You cannot accomplish on your own all that God wants to do in you. The decision to accept Jesus Christ as Lord and Savior is the greatest, most life-changing decision any individual will ever make. If you have never made that decision, you can do so right now. God is waiting with His arms outstretched for you to turn to Him and receive the new life He offers. The new birth is a simple process. Romans 10:9 says that if you confess with your mouth the Lord Jesus and believe in your heart that God has raised Him from the dead, you will be saved.

After becoming born again, the next biggest step is to find a church that teaches the uncompromised Word of God. It's essential that you find a place where you can be nourished and encouraged in your new walk. Why? The devil comes immediately to steal, kill and destroy and you make his job much easier when you are outside the protection of a Body of Christ that watches over your soul. God has given shepherds for His flock to care for you, but you need to submit yourself to their care. Get involved in the church where God leads you and begin to use the gifts He has given you.

PRAY THIS PRAYER:

> Heavenly Father, I realize I am a sinner and I need You in my life. I believe Jesus is the Son of God and that He took my place of punishment by dying on the cross. I ask Jesus to come and live within my heart, to lead me and guide me. I reject satan as my lord and his ways of sin, and I make Jesus Lord of my life. Thank you, God my Father, for accepting me as your child and saving me from eternal torment. I pray this in the Name of Jesus. Amen.

STUDY QUESTIONS

1. **Explain what II Corinthians 5:17 means in your own words.**

2. **Identify some areas in your life where you are being challenged right now and list them.**

3. Since we know that all things work together for good
    to those who love God and are called according to His
    purpose (Rom. 8:28), how do you think God can use
    the present trials you are facing?

CHAPTER THREE
YOUR GOD-GIVEN MINISTRY

People should be able to easily identify us as Christians by our lifestyle. Jesus said that they would know us by our fruit, our love for one another. That doesn't mean we won't struggle or get resistance from our flesh and our soul. The soulish man will rise up and say, "No, I want to do it my way." Jeremiah 17:9 says that man's heart (or in this case, soul) is "desperately wicked, who can know it?"We have a soul that wants to do everything but serve God!

However, we can also recognize our spirit man rising up: "Hey, wait a minute! Look what Jesus Christ did for me. How can I not serve and worship Him?" So there is always a tug of war going on between our soul and spirit. If you are not sensing this struggle I'm talking about, be concerned. We can fool some of the people some of the time (actually, we can fool all of the people all of the time if they only see us in church), but guess what? We can't fool Father God any of the time, never! We can come to church, dress up, play the part and spout the church lingo "Hallelujah, glory to God, praise the Lord" and still be on our way to hell. We can even learn to pray by parroting somebody else. If we're not careful, we can actually go to hell sitting in church!

We have certainly perfected the ability to play church. But we can do all the right church stuff and still miss heaven because we are not producing fruit that remains. We very rarely hear hard topics like forgiveness spoken about from the pulpit because churches don't want to lose members. They say, "Come on in. You're going to hell, but keep bringing your tithes and offerings. Are we entertaining you enough? Are your ears being tickled? No? No problem, we've got an even bigger "name" speaking here next week!" Churches have learned the fine art of being "seeker-sensitive" and not offending anybody. But how about being "Holy Spirit-sensitive"? Is He in attendance at our services? Do we care?

This is the sad state that the church finds itself in today because we are afraid to tell people the truth. If the truth were spoken, I believe that thousands who are just warming the pews would run down to the altar and get saved. Or they would stop pretending, get out of the church altogether and act like the sinners they really are. At least then God could truly save them by grace.

YOU'VE BEEN GIVEN A MINISTRY

But all things are from God, who through Jesus Christ, reconciled us to Himself, received us into His favor, brought us into harmony with Himself, and gave to us the ministry of reconciliation. (II Corinthians 5:18, Amplified Version)

We already looked at this scripture in the previous chapter, but I want to dig a little deeper. Notice that the ministry of reconciliation is now our ministry. God gave it to us. Having a whole relationship through the atonement, through redemption and through forgiving someone so that we can be one with them has become our ministry. Have you been looking for a ministry? Well, here it is! Just go find someone who hurt you (That may not be too hard, right?) and start ministering. Call somebody who has walked all over you and then wiped their feet on you and get into your ministry!

Over the years we've had many people tell us they are looking for their ministry. They want to find their purpose. They are looking for a "word" from a prophet that will unlock some secret revelation and direct them into their ministry. Of course, there is always someone willing to tell them that they are called to the nations and that they will minister to thousands!

As a Pastor, I am grieved that most "words" direct the focus away from building the local church and lead people to act like lone rangers. The only reason some people even stay involved in the local church is so they can use it as a springboard to launch their private ministry. That is an abuse of the Body of Christ! Some people are indeed called to go to the nations, and the local church should certainly send them. However, I am yet to hear anyone tell me they received a prophetic word to "Go and forgive your mother... or father... or husband... or wife.... Lay down your life for your family." No one seems to want to embrace the ministry of reconciliation, yet that is the one ministry to which God has called every one of us!

Of course, you cannot do it in your own strength. You need the Holy Spirit, the power of God, to help you impart forgiveness to others and lead the unsaved to God's forgiveness. (If you are born-again you can have the power of the Holy Spirit by simply asking the Father, in the name of Jesus for the Holy Spirit.) Do you understand God wants you to be Christ's ambassador? I think sometimes we are more satan's ambassadors than we are Christ's. It sounds cruel, but it's true.

God's heart is to restore us to unity with Himself and unity with one another. It is not a lone thing. It is a corporate thing. It's not just about you and *your* ministry. We must act as a corporate body, encouraging unity between brothers and sisters. He is *our* Father which art in heaven, hallowed be His name. He is not just *my* Father or just *your* Father. He is *our* Father.

I am the proud father of five grown children. They are all serving the Lord in ministry, and the spouses of the four who are married are also in ministry. As a father, nothing pleases me as much as seeing all my children getting along together, loving each other and helping each other. Of course, there are times when there are disagreements but, when they forgive each other quickly, I am especially blessed. I know that our heavenly Father, our Abba, feels the same way about His children. There is something about being connected with one another in a corporate body that reveals the fullness of who God is. It's something you or I can't do alone. That is why the devil works so hard to separate us and make us feel insignificant. He doesn't want to see God revealed.

The greatest force on the face of the earth is love, and love must include forgiveness. God poured His love inside of us. That means He has also poured inside of us the power to forgive. It is the very heart of God! I say this with tremendous zeal and passion because I know it is so critical to leading a victorious life. Yet I see so many Christians struggle with forgiving. They argue, "But you don't know what he did to me. You don't know what she said."

It has nothing to do with what he or she did. It has everything to do with what Jesus Christ did. He didn't forgive you because you turned your life around and became so sweet. He died on the cross to reconcile you to Him when you were still your same old miserable self. You didn't deserve it. None of us did, but He wanted to be united with us again. Now He has handed over to you the same ministry of reconciliation.

FORGIVENESS: THE CALL OF THE CHURCH

Forgiveness is what this Christian walk is all about— and not just forgiving someone for the sake of our own healing. We can't stress this point enough. Forgiveness is the foundation of all of Christianity. You've read my (Michele's) testimony, about how bitter I was. I almost didn't get saved. Do you know why? Because I knew that if I prayed the salvation prayer, I would have to forgive the people in my life who hurt me, and I didn't want to. I wanted to hold on to the anger. Isn't that ridiculous? Yet, we all do it. We hold on to hurts and refuse to forgive, thinking we're punishing the people who hurt us. God knows forgiveness is key to our redemption and spiritual growth, so He sent His Holy Spirit to enable and empower us to do it. Only He can touch our hearts and help us to release His forgiveness.

How are we going to win the world? Someone walks in the door on Sunday morning and they don't fit our "image" of what a good Christian should look like, so we give them the cold shoulder. Some churches like to get dressed to the hilt (and that's fine, nothing wrong with that), but when someone comes in wearing jeans and a tee-shirt, and we reject them, that's wrong. We have no right to put such conditions on people. We say, "You can come to church if you stop cursing and stop drugging and stop dressing like a whore and stop being a prostitute." If they could do all that, they wouldn't need you and they wouldn't need Jesus.

The truth is, when the world comes to church, they are supposed to see unconditional love. They are supposed to see this powerful force of forgiveness. That is our call. Why are the churches empty today? Why is the world running everywhere else for answers but the church? We need to take a good look at ourselves. We need to be freed from the religious mindset and its rigid thinking. *We always did it this way, so don't even think of changing anything, even if it means that someone will be blessed. Don't rock the boat.* The religious crowd even rebuked Jesus for healing on the Sabbath. They cared more about religious tradition than the flow of God's healing presence. That is why our churches have so many empty seats. **If we let the power of the Holy Spirit flow and impart love and forgiveness through us, I'm convinced Sunday mornings would be standing room only!**

Second Corinthians 5:20 calls the church ambassadors for Christ.

> *Now then, we are ambassadors for Christ as though God did beseech you by us, we pray you in Christ's stead be ye reconciled to God. (II Cor. 5:20)*

As ambassadors, we are called to the ministry of reconciliation. That's what ambassadors do—reach out on behalf of one kingdom or nation to others and promote unity and smooth over rough spots. We are called to express this powerful force of forgiveness on God's behalf and love those who are hurting, dying and on their way to hell. If we can't do it in our own homes—husbands forgiving wives, wives forgiving husbands, children forgiving parents, parents forgiving children—how in the world are we going to minister to people who do not even know God? If we can't even express forgiveness in the church, where one person gets upset with another person and one ministry gets upset with another ministry and the church splits, where is the nature of Christ? Church leadership needs to sit down with people and say "Wait a minute. What are you doing? You're behaving like a soulish, carnal Christian!"

Church, we have got to get out of our soulish Christianity (letting our emotions and ideas take precedent over the Word of God), and get into Spirit-led Christianity. That's where there's life. Following your feelings and opinions and the feelings and opinions of others only brings death and destruction. Someone has to tell the truth. Let's check ourselves. The church's call is to bring the message of unconditional love and unconditional forgiveness to those out there in the world. But, if we can't do it within our four walls, how are we going to do it out there?

It's amazing the attitudes we have with one another! It blows me away how the people in the Body of Christ treat each other. We talk so badly about each other, as though our side is better than their side. "They disappointed me. Don't you understand? It's *me* we're talking about. They disappointed *me*!" Oh yeah, we say "I forgive you," but we really don't forgive, and that's the truth. Human forgiveness says: "I will forgive you of the penalty, but I will never ever forget what you did to me. And I am not going to let you forget it either. I am never going to let go of these feelings."

Divine forgiveness says: "I do not care what you did. The price is paid, and with the help of God, I will never bring it back up to my memory again. And I will treat you as though it never happened, as though satan never tempted you to do what you did to me. I willfully choose to let it go." Folks, this is supernatural, and we do not have enough of it in the church today. Yet it's exactly what we need—unconditional love and unconditional forgiveness.

WALKING IN FORGIVENESS VS WALKING ON EGGSHELLS

We need a major paradigm shift in the Body of Christ wherein we show people mercy and compassion instead of judgment. We need to love them back into fellowship, rather than cutting them off. In reality, we in the church walk on eggshells with one another, because we know that if we make a mistake, it is all over. "That's it! I'm leaving the church! Did you hear what they said to me? Did you see how she looked at me?" Church, you and I have to shift the balance in the Kingdom of God.

When Word of Life Church first moved our world head-quarters from New York to Florida, everybody ran over here. We were the new show in town and many thought it would be the perfect place to advance their "spiritual career." But when they didn't get what they expected from us, they ran someplace else. Then when *that* church didn't tickle their fancy, they went to yet another church. Then finally they all stayed home and acted real spiritual: "I don't need church. I have God. It's just me, mine and I; and I can get along with myself real easy." Sure, you can. At home, there is nobody to challenge your miserable, selfish, self-centered ways.

On the other side of the fence, we see shepherds who are equally self-centered: "It's my way or the highway! You are here to advance *my* ministry and build *my* kingdom." Or they push people away by telling them they are too dys-functional, instead of flowing in mercy and compassion. That is also an abomination in the eyes of God!

The Apostle Paul compares the Body of Christ to the way the natural body functions. How healthy would your body be if some of the organs decided one day that they would not work and cooperate with the others? You would not be around for very long. Beloved, we need each other more than we are willing to admit. I need the gifts God placed in you and you need the gifts He placed in me. Yet we withhold from each other because of offenses, real or imagined. We opt out because, in order to walk in divine forgiveness, we have to crucify the flesh.

I'm telling you, **forgiveness is the key that unlocks the power of healing in your life!** It's the key that releases the power of God to bring revival on the face of the earth, and this is where God is taking the remnant—the few in the Church who have ears to hear, eyes to see and are willing to obey. And I believe it's where He is taking you and me, in the name of Jesus.

PRAY THIS PRAYER:

Dear Heavenly Father, help me to be a vessel through which your love, mercy and compassion can flow. As I learn to receive forgiveness from You, help me to release it to others. I want to fulfill my role here on earth as Christ's ambassador. Help me through the Holy Spirit to be sensitive to the needs of others and freely give forgiveness as I have freely received it. Thank you for allowing me to used by You in this way as You bring healing to Your creation. Amen.

STUDY QUESTIONS

1. **Think about people in your life to whom you need to minister reconciliation—reconciliation between them and God, you and them or them and other people.**

2. **How can forgiveness lead to a victorious life?**

3. Has anyone ever said they have to walk on eggshells around you? If so, how do you feel you can change this image?

4. On a separate sheet of paper, list anyone you have not forgiven and the offense(s) they committed against you. (Keep this list handy. You'll need it later.)

CHAPTER FOUR
HUMAN VS DIVINE FORGIVENESS

When God talks about forgiveness He means divine forgiveness, not human forgiveness. They are two very different things. There is a HUGE difference between divine forgiveness and human forgiveness.

Human forgiveness will not punish the person overtly, but will always remember what they did and find little ways to remind them of it. **Someone walking in human forgiveness never truly lets the person off the hook. However, the offense stays with the so-called forgiver too and binds them to the sin of unforgiveness.** As long as we move in human forgiveness, we will never experience full restoration.

God wants to restore our relationship with each other as well as with Him. He works both horizontally and perpendicularly, creating a perfect image of the cross. When we are restored to God (when we receive Jesus and are born again) then we can be restored to each other. When we begin to impart divine forgiveness, healing will take place in the Body of Christ, paving the way for revival in the Church. I'm not talking about the kind of revival that comes today and goes tomorrow, but revival that will take us into the second coming of Jesus. **True revival will come to a Body that understands forgiveness.** That is what God is doing in this hour.

Divine forgiveness recognizes that the debt was paid 2,000 years ago, and that the blood of Jesus Christ blotted out all sin. His blood cleansed us of sin. When we choose to truly forgive someone, we behave as though they never sinned, as though the incident never happened. We make a choice to look at them through the blood of Jesus Christ and through His eyes of love. That is God's divine forgiveness.

> *Who hath delivered us from the power of darkness, and hath translated us into the kingdom of his dear Son: In whom we have redemption through his blood, even the forgiveness of sins. (Colossians 1:13)*

God the Father redeemed or "bought us back" with the blood of His dear Son. It was an extremely high price that Jesus paid for us. He said, "My life for yours. Only receive My forgiveness."

GRACE! GRACE!

We have become religious instead of Christ-like. The Church has a form of godliness, but lacks the power. This is not a put-down, but rather a true evaluation. It's time to realize where we are. If we know where we are, we can figure out how to get where we need to go. God shows us that forgiveness is key. It's not an option. It is a command—one we can accomplish. Would God command us to do something He has not given us the power to do? We already have the ability to do it. However, we have to tap into divine forgiveness from our spirit rather than our soul. Our feelings, emotions, taste, sight, hearing, smell, logic, rationale, will never get us in touch with God. The only way to get in touch with God and apprehend this supernatural ability to forgive is through our born again spirit because God is Spirit. The Lord makes this message clear when He speaks to Zerubbabel through the prophet Zechariah:

> *Then he answered and spake unto me, saying, This is the word of the LORD unto Zerubbabel, saying, Not by might, nor by power, but by my spirit, saith the LORD of hosts. Who art thou, O great mountain? before Zerubbabel thou shalt become a plain: and he shall bring forth the headstone thereof with shoutings, crying, Grace, grace unto it. (Zechariah 4:6, 7)*

God called Zerubbabel to rebuild the Temple for Him. He has also called us to build a temple, a holy habitation, a dwelling place for God made without hands. It seemed like an impossible task, so Zerubbabel had to understand that his own works could not accomplish this goal. Every impossible task can only be done through the Spirit of God. Like Zerubbabel, we also are called to face a mountain—a mountain called unforgiveness. But, by the Spirit of God, that mountain will be flattened into a plain and we can extend grace to those we forgive! We can extend God's grace to others, just as He extended His grace to us when we were forgiven.

God asked us to receive His forgiveness. He wants to pour out His love to all mankind and He will do it through the Body of Christ. We are the extension of the heart of God to a world that is separated from His love. When you forgive somebody, the whole idea is to pour out the love of Christ to them. **Recognize that they can't see Christ for themselves, but they can see Him through you, by the grace of God.**

OBEDIENCE TAKES FAITH

We are put to the ultimate test to obey the command to forgive when the person we forgive does the same thing over and over again! That is where a true understanding of obedience comes in.

> *And if he trespass against thee seven times in a day, and seven times in a day turn again to thee, saying, I repent; thou shalt forgive him. And the apostles said unto the Lord, 'Increase our faith.'* (Luke 17:4, 5)

They were talking about obeying the command to forgive when they asked for an increase in faith. They knew how hard it was to obey. It is not about feelings. It is not because it feels right. It is accomplished by having faith in God's Word.

Obedience is better than sacrifice. We cannot bargain with God and do something else instead of obeying Him. Obedience obeys whether or not it agrees. We don't have to have a Board meeting, make a decision and then say, "God we think you're right so therefore, we are going to be obedient to you." He is the Chairman of the Board. What He says goes! He says, "Forgive!" End of story. We are slaves to God. We signed on the dotted line and there is only one position available on the application: slave. In Biblical days, people were often sentenced to serve as a slave for an appointed amount of time. When they repaid their debt to the master they could go free. At that point the slave could say, "You know, I have been a slave for six years and I choose to call you my master no matter what."

Over and over I hear Christians call Jesus King. The problem is that, in our culture, we do not understand the concept of living in a kingdom. We are accustomed to choosing and voting for our leadership, so we put God's authority in the same context. By definition a king has sovereign rule and reign over his kingdom and his subjects. Kings are not voted in or chosen. The king's subjects obey his laws and demands without question and often under penalty of death. This does not sound politically correct, does it? Well, if we serve the King of Kings and the Lord of Lords, shouldn't we be giving our unquestioning obedience and submission to Him? Do we have faith in Him and His Word to allow Him to be our Master, our Ruler, and our King? He commands us to forgive one another. Let's do it.

FORGIVE US AS WE FORGIVE

Forgive us our debts as we forgive our debtors. (Matthew 6:12)

Let's just say it this way: **Forgive us as we forgive.** As we forgive others, God is inclined to forgive us for our sins. When you don't forgive others, God holds back the forgiveness of your sins. Think about that for a moment. I wonder how many sins have piled up in our lives and remain unforgiven. We've been stubborn and rebellious, disobedient to God by not forgiving, thinking *It's okay. I'll get away with it because God loves me.* Understand that God loves us unconditionally according to His Word. **He doesn't love us outside of the Word, because there is no relationship outside of His Word.** He loves us according to His truth, and the truth that we know will set us free. One reason we find ourselves in a backslidden condition, doing things we stopped doing years ago, is because our hearts are hardened. Our sins are not forgiven because we are not forgiving those who have hurt and wounded us.

When we forgive, it benefits the person we forgive because a force is released that frees them from satan's grasp. It benefits us because God now has the liberty to forgive us. *"Forgive us... as we forgive...."* God will certainly for-

41

give us, but now we see that our forgiveness is connected to our obedience to Him. We reap what we sow and in like measures, according to Luke 6:38.

> *Give, and it shall be given unto you; good measure, pressed down, and shaken together, and running over, shall men give into your bosom. For with the same measure that ye mete withal it shall be measured to you again. (Luke 6:38)*

We can't bypass spiritual laws. We'd like to bypass them and make up our own idea of what Christianity is all about. Mark 11:25 clarifies what Matthew just said:

> *And when ye stand praying, forgive, if ye have aught against any: that your Father also which is in heaven may forgive you your trespasses. But if ye do not forgive, neither will your Father which is in heaven forgive your trespasses. (Mark 11:25)*

Can it be any plainer? God can't answer your prayers if you have something against somebody. You better forgive them. *"Forgive, if you have aught against any that your Father... in heaven may (**may**—He needs your permission) forgive you your trespasses."* Your obedience in forgiving others is the permission He needs to forgive you.

WALK THE TALK

First John 1:9 tells me that if I go to God and confess my sins, He is faithful and just to forgive me and cleanse me of all unrighteousness. However, if I did not forgive my wife for what she did last week, the sins I confessed before Him this morning are still on my account. Why? Because He didn't even hear me when I prayed. **If I am walking in disobedience and rebellion, He does not hear and He does not answer.** That does not mean I won't go to heaven, because God already made a decision He's going to take me to heaven. He knows I am a sinner saved by grace. But it affects my day-to-day life and keeps me from being free of the traps satan sets for me. Sin in my life gives the devil an open door to come in like a roaring lion. He is looking for people to add to his dinner menu.

Today, maybe it is you because you have sin that has not been forgiven. You think it is forgiven, but because of your stubbornness in not forgiving, you have cut off your blessing. No wonder you are getting angrier and more rebellious! No wonder you are starting to lean toward the world more than ever before! No wonder every now and then a foul word comes out of your mouth! Before you know it, the initial sin of unforgiveness has caused you to backslide completely.

You want to know why the Bible is not coming alive for you. There is no revival in your life, no miracles, no signs and wonders. **God is not a respecter of people. He is a respecter of His Word. When you walk the walk, and talk the talk, God's power will come forth in your life.**

And he said unto them, When ye pray, say, Our Father which art in heaven, Hallowed be thy name. Thy kingdom come. Thy will be done, as in heaven, so in earth. Give us day by day our daily bread. And forgive us our sins; for we also forgive every one that is indebted to us. And lead us not into temptation; but deliver us from evil. (Luke 11:2-4)

You pray not to be led into temptation and to be delivered from evil, but it applies only after you have forgiven others, including YOURSELF. The hardest person to forgive most of the time is you. Like Peter, we think we can serve God in our own strength. Instead, we fall, fail and get uptight, but we can't forgive ourselves. If you do not forgive yourself, there is no way you are going to be led out of temptation or delivered from evil. You cannot ask God to do these things for you while there is a wall of unforgiveness between you and Him.

> *Behold the Lord's hand is not shortened, that it cannot save, neither his ear heavy, that it cannot hear. But, your iniquities have separated between you and your God. And your sins have hid his face from you that he will not hear. (Isaiah 59:1, 2)*

Sin separates you from God. You can shout, but God won't hear you and His face will be hidden from you. We do not see the blessings coming into our lives so we get angry at God, at the preacher and everybody else instead of taking responsibility for our actions and making wise choices.

> *But your iniquities have separated between you and your God, and your sins have hid his face from you, that he will not hear. For your hands are defiled with blood, and your fingers with iniquity; your lips have spoken lies, your tongue hath muttered perverseness. (Isaiah 59:2, 3)*

Unforgiveness is like murder. "Blood" in this scripture refers to the "blood-guilt" in our hearts from the bitter roots of unforgiveness. The Book of Revelation says that no murderer will inherit the Kingdom of God. Murder starts with pre-meditation. When we refuse to forgive, we build a wall in hearts, not caring if the person get delivered or not. We are angry, self-righteous and have roots of bitterness. Unforgiveness poisons our hearts and is literally murder.

FORGIVENESS IS RETROACTIVE

Let me ask you a question: When did Jesus forgive you and take away your sins? Was it at the moment that you sinned? No, He forgave you 2,000 years ago. To be even more accurate, He forgave you before the foundation of the world. Ephesians 1:3 and 4 says:

Blessed be the God and Father of our Lord Jesus Christ, who hath blessed us with all spiritual blessings in heavenly places in Christ: According as he hath chosen us in him before the foundation of the world, that we should be holy and without blame before him in love. (Eph. 1:3, 4)

The price was paid 2,000 years ago by what Jesus did on Calvary, but God planned it long before He even created the world.

Who is the image of the invisible God, the firstborn of every creature: For by him were all things created, that are in heaven, and that are in earth, visible and invisible, whether they be thrones, or dominions, or principalities, or powers: all things were created by him, and for him: And he is before all things, and by him all things consist.

The New Living Translation says **"He existed before everything else began, and he holds all creation together."**

And he is the head of the body, the church: who is the beginning, the firstborn from the dead; that in all things he might have the preeminence. For it pleased the Father that in him should all fullness dwell; And, having made peace through the blood of his cross, by him to reconcile all things unto himself; by him, I say, whether they be things in earth, or things in heaven. And you, that were sometime alienated and enemies in your mind by wicked works, yet now hath he reconciled in the body of his flesh through death, to present you holy and unblameable and unreproveable in his sight. (Colossians 1:15-22, NLT)

Forgiveness is already here and available. It is a free gift that has already been purchased and given to us long before we accept it or even realize our need for it. We simply apprehend forgiveness when we recognize that we are sinners, repent for our sins and accept it in our hearts. It is already complete, already functioning and fulfilled in God.

Since God's forgiveness is retroactive, so-to-speak, so should ours be for one another. That means that you and I should be walking around ready to forgive at all times. When you step on my toes the response should be: "I've already forgiven you." I shouldn't have to work it up by fasting and praying for five weeks, and then *maybe* I can somehow acquire the ability to forgive you. When you walk in divine forgiveness, you already have it dwelling inside you; you already have the power and the revelation. You already have the engrafted word in your heart that says:

> ...*forgive, if ye have aught against any: that your Father also which is in heaven may forgive you your trespasses. (Mark 11:25)*

You already have the nature of Jesus which is to forgive. **When people hurt you, if you're a Christian, forgiveness should be automatic.** This really is a supernatural concept. It is divine forgiveness.

A CRACK IN THE FOUNDATION

Human forgiveness says: "I won't punish you, but I am sure going to hold on to the hurt and the pain and the memory." When you ask a Christian, "Did you forgive your mother and father?" they say, "Sure, I forgave them." Maybe they did, humanly speaking. But, divinely? Because most of us have never understood the difference between divine forgiveness and human forgiveness, we continue to resurrect the past. Even though the incident happened thirty, forty or seventy years ago, it's still in the present if we carry it in our memory. The longer we hold on to it, the more deeply it becomes engraved in our thoughts and feelings, and satan will still be able to push those buttons and get a rise out of us whenever he wants to. The devil will put someone in your path to pick that scab until the old wound starts to bleed again.

Why? Because you have not truly forgiven that 30-year-old offense. You forgave as much as humanly possible, but the pain, the memory, the anguish, the scar is still there. The exact details might have disappeared from memory long ago but, the fact is, that wound is like a crack in the foundation upon which your life is built. Therefore your house is wobbly and, from time to time, you come tumbling down.

FORGIVENESS IS FORGETFULNESS

Isaiah 43:25 says

I, even I, am he that blotteth out thy transgressions.

God totally abolishes our sins. To divinely forgive is to totally do away with the wrong. God did it by shedding His own precious blood. We can't do that, but we can certainly do away with the offense by sacrificing our own feelings and desires, by appropriating the blood of Christ and reconciling the person through forgiveness. We can *choose* to forget what they did and abolish it from our mind every time we're reminded of it so that it won't influence how we treat that person in the future. I don't know how you feel about this but I know that, for myself, this is an almost impossible thing to do. It completely goes against the natural man's way of thinking. Most of us can forgive in a human way, but rarely do we forgive in a divine way because it is such a battle for us.

I, even I, am he that blotteth out thy transgressions for my own sake…

Notice *why* God blots out our transgressions. He does it for His own sake, not ours.

…and will not remember thy sins. (Isaiah 43:25)

47

I believe that every time we achieve this supernatural forgiveness in our relationships, it brings glory to God because we do it for His sake. That's what gives me the motivation to even want to forgive. Again in Chapter 44, God renews His promise to erase our sins and take us back:

I have blotted out as a thick cloud, thy transgressions, and, as a cloud, thy sins: return unto me; for I have redeemed thee. (Isaiah 44:22)

Our transgressions or sins are like a thick cloud hanging over our heads, but He chooses to wipe them from memory as if satan never enticed us and we never did what he told us to do. It is as though the devil was never in our garden and we never fell into sin. It's like it never happened, ever. Hallelujah! That is how God chooses to look at us. That does not mean we are perfect. It means He is perfect.

When we forgive somebody, it does not mean that they are perfect. It means that we are looking at them through the eyes of the only perfect One, Christ. None of us has arrived. We might be a little better off than we were two years ago, but we still have faults. Some of us have more than others, but we have been accepted in the Beloved, even with all our faults. Hallelujah! As we diligently seek God and get closer to Him, His light shines even brighter in our lives. That is very good news. However, there is a flip side to this as I have discovered over the years.

HIDDEN FAULT LINES

As I (Gaspar) grew and matured in the Lord there would be seasons of personal breakthroughs and I would sigh with relief, glad that the battle was over. That is an easy place to stay and camp out, but God is always on the move, always wanting to shine His light a little deeper into our souls. His light would always search out the next issue I had to deal with, the next person I needed to forgive. When the light in the secret places of my soul was dim, things seemed pretty clean. But when the Spirit of God came closer with the lamp (the Word) of God and flooded the place with light, all of a sudden I saw things I never saw before. God is so gracious. He never shines the spotlight everywhere at once. He goes to one place at a time, one issue at a time. Be careful though, because the enemy likes to overwhelm you with other layers of faults you have to deal with and make you think you can never get it right. **Tell the devil that you are going to praise the Lord, because He loves you enough to want to change you!** Don't ever think you have arrived, especially in the area of forgiveness. There can be additional layers, hidden areas, you don't know about yet, but neither should you condemn yourself.

I have blotted out as a thick cloud, thy transgressions, and, as a cloud, thy sins: return unto me; for I have redeemed thee. (Isaiah 44:22)

Listen to the Father God's heart. He wants you to come to Him. That is the heart we should have for those around us. We should want to draw them back into relationship. Say "I want to relate to you and be one with you. I want to walk life's journey with you. I want to be loved and love you like Christ loves me. Let's bury the hatchet and cleanse our sins with the blood of Jesus Christ. Let's stop pointing fingers at our problems and faults. Let's get beyond that and love each other."

That is God's power working inside of us. **The people He places in your life are divine appointments to bring out in you what you can't bring out yourself.** God won't always surround you with nice people. He'll give you grumpy, angry, selfish people so you can love them into

49

submission. You say, "Why me, God?" He says, "Why not you?" He chose you because He knows the ability and power He has placed in you.

You cannot give what you do not have, but if you have Jesus, you have what it takes. Tell yourself, "I have what it takes." I don't care how mean and grumpy your spouse is. You can forgive. The love of God will grab the meanest most ornery man or woman and bring them to their knees, bring tears to their eyes and bring them into a love relationship with Him. God's love, God's power of forgiveness, will never fail. Never! Remember it is the goodness of God that leads to repentance.

FORGIVENESS FORE-GIVES

Psalm 103:11,12 says:

For as the heaven is high above the earth, so great is His mercy toward them that fear him. As far as the east is from the west, so far hath he removed our transgressions from us. (Psalm 103:11, 12)

East and west never meet, never. He throws all of our sins into the sea of forgetfulness and posts a sign that says "No Fishing". It is never brought up again. No one is supposed to bring it up again. So when we forgive somebody in a divine way, we no longer bring it up to them or anyone else (including God). We no longer treat them as though they did anything wrong. Think about this. We can really press in, decide to follow God's Word and forgive someone, really, really forgive them. It is actually a satisfying feeling when we offer true divine forgiveness. We feel free and know that we have done the right thing in God's eyes. It is quite an accomplishment. So, we go along our merry way, walking in the victory.

However, something often happens that we didn't count on. The person we forgave turns around and does the same thing to us again, or even worse! Then what? "God, you certainly don't expect me to go through the same process all over again, do you? No way, now I know that they didn't even appreciate or deserve the forgiveness in the first place!" I think something like this went through Peter's mind when he questioned Jesus in Matthew 18:21 and 22:

> *Then came Peter to him, and said, Lord, how oft shall my brother sin against me, and I forgive him? till seven times? Jesus saith unto him, I say not unto thee, Until seven times: but, Until seventy times seven. (Matthew18:21, 22)*

We forgive them again because forgiveness is really fore-giveness. We give it beforehand. So if they do it again, we must forgive them again… and again… and again. How many times do we forgive them? Jesus makes it very clear, so clear, in fact, that we are now without excuse. How many times has God forgiven us? Let's face it. We have all committed sins over and over and over, even the same ones, even after we were forgiven. Forgiveness is forever. It is unconditional. There is no limit. Forgiveness is an attitude and a lifestyle, not just a one-time thing. **Giving beforehand defines true forgiveness.** Be prepared to forgive that person even before they do anything wrong so that, when it happens, you do not have to work it up. It is already inside of you. It is your nature—God's nature.

We say, "Okay, that's it! I've forgiven you 20 times and that's where I draw the line!" We are not God. Look at yourself in the mirror and realize how many times you have blown it. Yet, God does not knock on your door and remind you of your past, does He? When God talks to us, it is not about the past. God always talks destiny. He talks about where He is taking us and the great things He has in store for us. He talks about the health and prosperity He bought and paid for us. That is "God language". We need to learn to speak as He speaks.

PROOF YOU ARE HIS

It is proof positive that you are His when you bear the fruit of forgiveness. Anyone who doesn't live a lifestyle of forgiveness does not have the nature of Jesus in them, and they need to get saved. Do you understand that you can mentally ascent to Jesus Christ as Lord and Savior? I am not saying that you are perfect every day or that you forgive everybody right away, but the proof is in the pudding. The proof is in the fruit. You know the tree by its fruit, and the very nature of God is forgiveness.

If you have God's nature, His nature should govern your lifestyle. Yours should be a life evidenced by extreme compassion and mercy—not because it is your natural tendency, but—because it is Christ's nature that flows through you. Amen? **In fact, because it is *not* human nature to forgive, the world will clearly see that there is something different about you.** They will see God's divine nature and it will appeal to them. Then God will get the glory and His name will be hallowed! By your very lifestyle, you will lift up Jesus, the Son of man, and He will draw all men to Him.

Understand me. You might get uptight and angry and have a "hallelujah breakdown" once in a while but, for the most part, when you have God's nature flowing through you, you walk in the Spirit and not in the flesh. It is best that I tell you the truth so that, if you are not saved yet, you will realize it and get saved. Today is your day of salvation!

And ye shall seek me, and find me, when ye shall search for me with all your heart. (Jeremiah 29:13)

It would be a horrible thing to go to heaven, stand before the Lord and hear Him say, "You're not really saved. Depart from Me. I never knew you." He will remind you that you never forgave your husband.

"But You don't know, Lord. You don't understand."

"I don't understand? I am God. I knew the worst thing you would ever do before you did it, and I still gave My life for you. I gave you the power to be My ambassador, to represent Me in heaven and on earth. This was your call. I did not expect those I called to walk in human forgiveness, I gave them the power to walk in *My* forgiveness."

FRUIT THAT REMAINS

When your life overflows with divine forgiveness and unconditional love as it should, this is simply a manifestation of a born again spirit. John 15:16 says:

Ye have not chosen me, but I have chosen you, and ordained you, that ye should go and bring forth fruit, and that your fruit should remain. (John 15:16)

Do you see that? What kind of fruit is He talking about? You may think that He means that we should go and spread the Gospel and get people saved. Yes, that is true. But He is also talking about something deeper. You cannot truly get someone saved without the nature of Christ in you bringing forth the ministry of reconciliation in the power of God's grace and mercy by the Holy Spirit.

No man can say that Jesus is the Lord, but by the Holy Ghost. (I Corinthians 12:3)

Natural babies require natural conception. Spiritual babies (or spiritual fruit) require supernatural conception.

There must also be supernatural birth, and it cannot happen unless supernatural power is flowing through us.

Ye have not chosen me, but I have chosen you…. (John 15:16)

Isn't that wonderful? You say you found the Lord, but He was never lost—you were. **The Lord knew exactly where He was. He was just trying to get your attention, so you would know where you are.**

In the Garden of Eden after the fall God said, "Where art thou, Adam?"

Do you think God didn't know where Adam was? He just wanted Adam to recognize his plight, his desperate condition, and say "I'm lost, Lord. I'm naked. I'm looking at everything through my feelings and emotions, and now I am trying to cover myself up with a billion excuses. I put on a fig leaf, but now it's dying; so I'm going to have to exchange the excuses for something else real quick."

"Where art thou, Adam?"

"I am lost, Lord, and on my way to hell… and I'm bitter and angry with my wife."

As with Adam, God wants you to know where you are in your Christian walk. He wants you to understand that you have just begun the journey. He still has to heal your soul, then your body and your relationships. Your first step in that journey is to forgive.

TRUE LOVE

First John 4:7 says,

Beloved, let us love one another: for love is of God; and everyone that loveth is born of God, and knoweth God. He that loveth not…

Or we could say "forgiveth not unconditionally".

...knoweth not God; for God is love. (I John 4:7)

The word used here for love is *agapao*: unconditional love. It is a divine, God-inspired kind of love. **Love demands forgiveness.** To forgive is to walk in unconditional love. It is unconditional because you are not looking for anything in return. You are not expecting the person forgiven to do anything like make amends or make things right. Sure, it would be good if they did make things right but, as for you, your part is to present to them the gift of forgiveness—no strings attached.

If you're acting in agapao (unconditional, divine love and unconditional forgiveness), then you can know for sure that you are born of God. You are born again or born from above. It is not a guessing game. Loving by forgiving is the way to know for sure where you stand with God. He who does not forgive does not know God. It is that simple. If you love, you know God. If you do not love, you do not know God. If you do not operate in divine forgiveness, then you know that you do not know God, because God is love.

In this was manifested the love of God toward us, because that God sent his only begotten Son into the world, that we might live through him. (I John 4:9)

How was the love of God manifested? By sending His only begotten Son into the world that we might live through Him.

For God so loved the world that He gave His only begotten Son... (John 3:16)

Herein is love, not that we loved God, but that He loved us, and sent His Son to be the propitiation for our sins. (I John 4:10)

Jesus was the propitiation or atoning sacrifice for us. He became our redemption, the price paid for us so our sins could be forgiven. We ought to be paying for our own sins, but He said "I will pay the price for you." Did you deserve it? No, but He chose to love you and bring you to Himself so He could have a relationship with you. Why did He save you? To bring you to Himself. Why did He deliver you? To bring you to Himself. Why did He set you free from the sins that were binding you up and sending you to hell? To bring you to Himself so that He could have a love relationship with you. Now why do we run to everything else but God? Why is He still the last One we call on? Why do we still struggle with spending time with Him? Why do we still complain to Him? Do we understand what He has done for us?

VENGEANCE IS HIS, NOT YOURS

Since God is asking us to do something that He is also giving us the power to do, we do not have a right to hold back. Of course, our enemy the devil will blind our minds and make us feel that if we forgive somebody, we are letting them off the hook. But, it is not our concern to keep them on the hook or let them off; it is God's business, not ours. Since He has forgiven *us* and let *us* off the hook, we are to take the same ministry and forgive others so they can come into the saving knowledge of Jesus Christ.

> *Recompense to no man evil for evil. Provide things honest in the sight of all men. If it be possible, as much as lieth in you, live peaceably with all men. Dearly beloved, avenge not yourselves, but rather give place unto wrath: for it is written, Vengeance is mine; I will repay, saith the Lord. Therefore if thine enemy hunger, feed him; if he thirst, give him drink: for in so doing thou shalt heap coals of fire on his head. Be not overcome of evil, but overcome evil with good.* (Romans 12:17-21)

This scripture makes it very clear. No matter what a person does to us, we are not to repay them with evil. In fact, we are to do everything possible to live in peace with them, taking it to the limit. When we want revenge we have to remember that God says He is the one who will take care of it. Then, to make matters worse, not only does He say that we cannot take revenge, He says that we have to be nice to them. We have to feed them and give them something to drink! As we do good, it will overcome their evil! There are some verses in the Bible that we wish we could blot out and, for most of us, this is one of them. There is nothing here that appeals to the flesh!

One reason it's so hard to forgive is because our flesh wants revenge. Something in our carnal, lustful, self-centered nature wants to retaliate. That is why there are so many successful movies based on getting revenge. "Get 'em back! Kill 'em!" Sure we go to church on Sunday, but they deserve everything that they get! The whole thing appeals to the flesh, that sin nature, an eye for an eye, a tooth for a tooth. You hurt me; I will hurt you back. You are not getting away with anything.

We will always find a way to justify our position. We do not want to deal with the issue. We say, "I go to church, give my tithes and offerings and bless the Lord. Do not talk to me about this issue. I have been hurt. You do not understand how I have been hurt."

WE NEED THE HOLY SPIRIT

Feelings and emotions in themselves are not wrong or right; it just depends on who is leading them, who is lord over them. We need to experience the baptism of the Holy Spirit and of fire. Why? Because **the baptism of fire brings passionate love for God and for the things of God. We**

57

will love what God loves and hate what God hates. It can be discouraging to try to bring our feelings and emotions under the Lordship of Jesus Christ. We need the Holy Spirit more than we can imagine! The Holy Spirit is key to living a victorious Christian life, so let us learn more about Him.

Being born again prepares us to receive the Holy Spirit. He is the power, the *dunamis*. He is the "ability" of God. We need to be baptized in the Holy Spirit, evidenced by divine forgiveness flowing through our lives. Being born again but not baptized with the Holy Spirit, means we are on our way to heaven but we will not be very effective against the works of darkness.

Here is an example of being born again versus being born again and filled with the Holy Spirit: Being born again is like trying to put out a house fire with buckets. We get one bucket and have to run back and pour it on the house. By the time we go back and forth three times, the house is burnt down. Being baptized with the Holy Spirit means we are holding a hose that is hooked up to a fire hydrant that provides a powerful, steady stream of water. We point it toward the fire, stand firm and we have all the power we need to put it out!

In the book of Acts Jesus told His disciples:

But ye shall receive the power after that the Holy Ghost has come upon you. (Acts 1:8)

First the Holy Spirit comes upon us and then the power comes; our born again spirit prepares us to be baptized in the Holy Spirit.

Luke 3:21-23 says:

Now when all the people were baptized, it came to pass, that Jesus also being baptized, and praying, the heaven was opened, And the Holy Ghost descended in a bodily shape like a dove upon him, and

a voice came from heaven, which said, Thou art my beloved Son;
in thee I am well pleased. And Jesus himself began to be about
thirty years of age.

Luke 4:1,2a says:

And Jesus being full of the Holy Ghost returned from Jordan, and
was led by the Spirit into the wilderness. Being forty days tempt-
ed of the devil.

Our Savior Jesus received the Holy Spirit when John the
Baptist baptized Him in the Jordan River. Satan's attack was
the first thing He experienced after being baptized in the
Holy Spirit. We are familiar with the encounter between
Jesus and satan in the wilderness, and know that Jesus
overcame temptation. It is important to pay attention to
details when we study scripture. Look at the time sequence
of the previous passage. Before Jesus faced satan He
received the power of the Holy Spirit. What does that tell
us? Do you think that maybe before we battle satan we
need to be empowered by the Holy Spirit too?

It is our Father's good pleasure to give us the Holy
Spirit. At the end of this chapter, we will lead you in a
prayer to be empowered by the Holy Spirit so that, by His
grace, you can accomplish this divine forgiveness.

Whatsoever you desire, when you pray, believe that you receive
and ye shall have it. (Acts 10:43)

GOD'S WORD VS MAN'S PHILOSOPHY

Part of the problem is that we are always trying worldly techniques. We are constantly bombarded by the philoso-
phies of the world. Every talk show, reality show, movie
and self-help book tells us that they have the answers to our
unhappy marriage or our depression or our (you name it)!

You name a problem and there is someone out there in the media willing to show you the way (usually with a price tag attached), and their way is almost always against God's Word and His ways. Unfortunately, even in Christian book stores and media outlets you are flooded with man's philosophy.

> *Beware lest any man spoil you through philosophy and vain deceit, after the tradition of men, after the rudiments of the world, and not after Christ. For in him dwelleth all the fullness of the Godhead bodily. And ye are complete in him, which is the head of all principality and power. (Colossians 2:8-10)*

Paul is saying that, **in Christ, we are complete because Jesus has authority over every principality and power that is causing all our problems.** No man can offer a better deal than that!

> *Blessed is the man that walketh not in the counsel of the ungodly, nor standeth in the way of sinners, nor sitteth in the seat of the scornful. (Psalm 1:1)*

God wants you instead to delight yourself in the Word of the living God. Then, according to Psalm 1:3, you'll be like a tree planted by the rivers of water that brings forth your fruit in your season. We may start out just walking in the counsel of the ungodly but, as you can see, there is a progression. The next thing we know, we are standing, hanging around in the way of the sinner. Finally, we find ourselves sitting with the scornful. Other translations substitute the word "scoffer" (someone who mocks or shows contempt) for the Word of God. So we actually end up agreeing with those who mock, ridicule and deny God's Word. The devil is sneaky. Instead, we are to delight ourselves in the Word of the living God. Then we will be like a tree that is prosperous and full of life, constantly drinking from God's river, bearing fruit and staying healthy. Why would we look anywhere else?

Yet, we have walked away. It is amazing how many people have the Bible, read the Bible, but still do not believe the Bible! I am talking about church people! It's amazing how many of us run to counselors instead of running to the rivers of living water in God's Word. Counselors only give us their own philosophical understanding of God's Word. **Man cannot interpret God. Only God can interpret God.**

> *If any of you lack wisdom, let him ask of God, that giveth to all men liberally, and upbraideth not; and it shall be given him. But let him ask in faith, nothing wavering. For he that wavereth is like a wave of the sea driven with the wind and tossed. For let not that man think that he shall receive any thing of the Lord. A double minded man is unstable in all his ways. (James 1:5-8)*

A double-minded man doesn't put his faith in God's Word. He listens to man instead. That is the problem with theology. It is man's study of God. Think about it: a man with a finite mind trying to study an infinite God. That does not make sense. **We can only know God through revelation.** He has to reveal His will to you, and He wants to. That is what He is trying to do through this book. He wants you to understand that the way to success, prosperity, and peace in your life is through forgiveness. The world will tell you the opposite: "Don't let people take advantage of you! Stand up for your rights." There are groups that advocate women's rights, men's rights, animal rights, etcetera, etcetera. I cannot believe the stuff that passes for godly counsel, and among Christians in churches! Guess what? You don't have rights. You gave them up when you gave your life to Christ. You took on His rights which was to lay Himself on the cross and die. It's your right to die too, for Jesus. Hallelujah! What an honor it is to die for Jesus.

STOP PLAYING GOD

And be ye kind one to another, tenderhearted, forgiving one another, even as God for Christ's sake hath forgiven you. (Ephesians 4:32)

This scripture tells us that the way to be kind, the way to be tenderhearted to one another and thereby fulfill this command is by forgiving one another. I can't be kind or have a tender heart to someone until I have forgiven them. It makes sense, but it is very difficult to forgive the way that God has forgiven us. It is a command, not a suggestion. Divine forgiveness is a command, not a choice.

We do not own forgiveness just as we do not own God's love. He has given it to us to be a good steward over. We say by our actions, "I am going to choose who to love this week." Or "I do not think that person deserves to be loved like Christ loved me. I don't think that person should be forgiven." We may not say these words consciously but we sure say them in our hearts. Who do we think we are? Church, this is the problem. **We have a distorted view of ourselves and we have become too big in our own eyes.** As long as we stay small in our own estimation, God will be the great and awesome God that He is and everything else will be in its correct perspective. Remember all the issues that we have had with people, issues that have added up over five, ten, fifteen years. We may have forgotten about most of these incidents, but they are still inside of us, still affecting our life and our decisions. That is because we have not taken the command to forgive seriously and given it the priority it should have.

We must forsake our own rights so Christ can claim His rights in the people we are forgiving. Now, I am not saying that if your spouse or someone else is physically abusing you or treating you horrendously you should stay in the relationship. You can forgive them while you are separated. You don't have to stay in their presence. But when those of us who are in the Lord refuse to walk in unconditional forgiveness and hold others to a higher standard of holiness and righteousness than we are willing to live up to ourselves, we are playing God. That puts us in a very dangerous place. God is not sleeping. He is not a gray-bearded benevolent grandpa in a rocking chair. He is not looking down into our giant playpen saying, "Just let them play. I don't care what they do. I will still take them to heaven one day." No, **God is saying, "What are you doing with My love?... and the forgiveness My Son bled and died to secure for you, what are you doing with it?"** It is proof positive that we are His when we flow in His divine forgiveness.

SIX REASONS TO FORGIVE

Below, we've quickly summed up some of the consequences of unforgiveness that we've discussed at length in this chapter.

1. **Unforgiveness keeps our sins from being forgiven.**

2. **Unforgiveness separates us from God.**

3. **Unforgiveness gives satan free access to our lives.**

4. **Unforgiveness takes us out of the will of God.**

5. **Unforgiveness hinders our faith.**

6. **Unforgiveness hinders our prayers.**

I've said it before and I will say it again, forgiveness is the call of the Church! Let's answer the call!

PRAY THIS PRAYER:

Father God, I ask You now to baptize me with the Holy Spirit and fire, evidenced by divine forgiveness and a free flow of Your love. I know that You give freely to all who ask, so I thank You for charging my spirit now with Your *dunamis* power to accomplish what I cannot in my limited human ability. Thank You, Holy Spirit, for filling me with the love of Jesus. Continue to stir up His compassion and mercy in me towards others so that I may glorify God in my attitudes and actions. Help me to forget the hurts that were done to me so that I can be effective in God's Kingdom. Use me with anyone and everyone, especially those who have hurt me the most. I know with You nothing is impossible. Amen.

STUDY QUESTIONS

1. What are some differences between human forgiveness and divine forgiveness?

2. What are some things that make it impossible to forgive in our human strength?

3. According to what you have learned, why do you *not* have the right to withhold forgiveness?

CHAPTER FIVE
GOD HAS A DESTINY FOR YOU

Then the word of the LORD came unto me, saying, Before I formed thee in the belly I knew thee; and before thou camest forth out of the womb I sanctified thee, and I ordained thee a prophet unto the nations.

Then said I, Ah, Lord GOD! behold, I cannot speak: for I am a child. But the LORD said unto me, Say not, I am a child: for thou shalt go to all that I shall send thee, and whatsoever I command thee thou shalt speak. Be not afraid of their faces: for I am with thee to deliver thee, saith the LORD.

Then the LORD put forth his hand, and touched my mouth. And the LORD said unto me, Behold, I have put my words in thy mouth. See, I have this day set thee over the nations and over the kingdoms, to root out, and to pull down, and to destroy, and to throw down, to build, and to plant. (Jeremiah 1:4-10)

We started this chapter with this awesome scripture because, as children of God, we must get a very important concept deeply rooted into our hearts so that we can withstand the many trials we must go through. To sum it up in one phrase: **We need a sense of destiny!** If you believe that you were just dropped here on earth by accident and you should wander around aimlessly until the

Lord calls us home, then you'll be easily defeated by the enemy. You will not be willing to pursue high goals in God, and you will see no purpose in living by the Spirit.

DEVELOP A SENSE OF DESTINY

As the Lord showed Jeremiah, He gave you and me a purpose before we were even conceived in our mother's womb. In the next verse, the prophet argued with God (like we often do) and said that he couldn't possibly do what He called him to do. God simply reiterated His call to destiny, while reassuring Jeremiah that He was with him. God then touched the mouth of the man who was destined to be one of the greatest prophets ever known, released supernatural ability and again stressed the great destiny He had planned for him. The Lord emphasized Jeremiah's destiny three times in one paragraph, He wasn't fooling around, was He?

In Psalm 139, King David also realized that God had a destiny for him before he was born.

> For thou hast possessed my reins: thou hast covered me in my mother's womb. I will praise thee; for I am fearfully and wonderfully made: marvellous are thy works; and that my soul knoweth right well. My substance was not hid from thee, when I was made in secret, and curiously wrought in the lowest parts of the earth. Thine eyes did see my substance, yet being unperfect; and in thy book all my members were written, which in continuance were fashioned, when as yet there was none of them. How precious also are thy thoughts unto me, O God! how great is the sum of them! (Psalm 139:13-17)

He knew that man's destiny was so important to God that He wrote it down in His book! He says God thinks about us constantly. Imagine that! God's thoughts are directed to us constantly and there are so many thoughts about us we cannot even count them! That shows that God obviously cares very much about our destiny, and maybe we should too. God has a destiny specifically for you!

The Bible tells us that Jesus had a destiny as well. It was to come to earth expressly to die. He was the sacrificial Lamb, sent to earth for us, so our sins could be forgiven.

> *But with the precious blood of Christ, as of a lamb without blemish and without spot: Who verily was foreordained before the foundation of the world, but was manifest in these last times for you. (I Peter 1:19,20)*

While He was here, Jesus did great works, but He made an astounding statement about those works. Jesus told His disciples (which includes us) that they would do greater works than He did.

> *Verily, verily, I say unto you, He that believeth on me, the works that I do shall he do also; and greater works than these shall he do; because I go unto my Father. (John 14:12)*

What was the greatest thing Jesus did? He made a way for us to be forgiven. **Since we know that God changeth not, and that He does not respect one person over another, we can definitely conclude that He has a divine purpose for our life.** Maybe you were not called to be a prophet like Jeremiah or a King like David, but you were called to do greater works! You were called to have the character of Christ. You were called to be a minister of reconciliation, walking in divine forgiveness. And you were called to walk in this destiny since before you were even conceived!

GOD WON'T ATTEND YOUR PITY PARTY

In Judges Chapter 6, we see Gideon living in fear and bondage because the Midianites were oppressing the

Israelites. He was hiding from the enemy when the angel of the Lord came to him and said:

> *The Lord is with thee, thou mighty man of valour.... Go in this thy might, and thou shalt save Israel from the hand of the Midianites: have not I sent thee?... Surely I will be with thee, and thou shalt smite the Midianites as one man. (Judges 6:12, 14, 16)*

Mighty man of valor?!! That's not quite how we would have described Gideon or even how he would have described himself. When we are down and out, struggling, oppressed and depressed, ready to quit, who wants to hear "The Lord is with thee, thou mighty man of valour"? We just want God to agree with us that our circumstances are horrible. I can tell you from experience, God does not cater to pity parties! However, you will not be alone. The devil will certainly show up and he will bring the food! He will invite others to sit with you, people who would rather eat satan's lies than dine on God's Truth.

We want God to tell us how He will beat up everybody that hurt us. We want Him to pat us on the back and say, "Oh there, there dear poor thing, everything is going to be okay one day." But God will not do that. **He will not talk to you about your history of misery. He will not talk about your present condition. He only talks about your destiny, your future.** He only talks about what He's done for you and where He's already taken you in your victory. He wants you to see the vision He has for you.

> *Where there is no vision, the people perish. (Proverbs 29:18a)*

In this verse, perish means "amount to nothing." God wants to instill in us *His* vision.

In Judges 6:12-16, Gideon argued back and forth with God about why he couldn't do what He was calling him to do. He wanted to talk to God about where he was. God refused. He told Gideon where He had taken him from and where He was going to take him—victory. God did not agree with the impossible circumstances. In fact, He made them even more impossible by eliminating most of Gideon's army, leaving him just a handful of men to go up against a huge enemy.

The same things happen to us. Sometimes when we decide to crucify the flesh and walk in God's divine forgiveness toward someone in our life, just as we begin to go forward flowing in His agape love, the person gets even meaner and nastier. Just remember, what seems impossible for us is possible for God! **Gideon had the power to fulfill his destiny and so do we.**

GET BRAIN-WASHED

God wants to talk to us today about our destiny in Him. Let's get rid of this woe-is-me, everybody-is-against-me, if-anything-bad-happens-it'll-happen-to-me victim mentality. It's negative and it opens the door for satan. The problem is that we often don't want to hear the truth. If we tape-recorded our reaction to someone who tells us the truth, we see that we get uptight and angry. We only want to talk about *our* circumstances, *our* hurt, *our* pain and it just begets more hurt and pain. What we sow is what we reap. If we keep talking about the problems, we will keep getting problems. We own them, even calling them ours. That is how satan sets up the assignment over our lives to perpetuate the same scenarios with different people, in different circumstances and in different geographical areas; but it's the same situation over and over again. Get rid of the victim mentality!

God told Gideon about the victory He already gave him. Even though he didn't look like he had it at that moment, God was saying, "Don't look at what you have now. Look at Me. Set your affections on Me." We have to renew our minds by getting into the Word and get brain-washed. Many years ago I (Gaspar) was told that if I went to church too much, I was going to get brainwashed. I realized that I was getting brainwashed everyday anyway. Every time I watched a TV commercial or read the newspaper, my brain was being washed by the world's ways. I simply chose what I wanted to wash my brain with. I decided to wash it with the water of God's Word; and that is what we need to do. If we don't wash our souls with the Word of God, the devil will wash it with negative circumstances. **Choose to be brainwashed by God.**

As a man thinks in his heart, so shall he be. (Proverbs 23:7)

Satan is always trying to build strongholds in our mind. If he can control our minds, he can control our destiny. But Jesus is our prototype. Whatever He does, we can do. What He overcomes, we can overcome, because we are made in His image. If we understand who we are in Christ, then we can use all the negative circumstances as springboards to catapult us above the problems into the eye of the storm where there is calm and peace. We can make it because Jesus has already made it. *If God is for me, who can prosper against me?* Stop waiting for the other shoe to drop and let's renew our mind with the Word of God. It takes discipline. God won't force us to let go of our past. We don't want to stay married to our past. If we let go of it, the past loses its power to hold us back. It will not stick to us. It will fall to the ground. **We can make the choice today to see, think, speak, act and re-act from a new mind—the mind of Christ.**

FROM MISERY TO MINISTRY

God will not lead us out of problems and into nothingness or cause us to wander aimlessly through the wilderness. He has a plan for delivering us. He takes us from our worst problems into greatness. The Lord told Abraham that He would make his name great, and we are heirs to Abraham's promise. God will do great things in your life if you let Him. God has preordained from the foundation of the world a great destiny for you. But if you do not agree with Him in it, it will not happen. He is taking you out of the mess in order to bless you; bringing you from misery into ministry. He has great things planned for you.

> *For the which cause I also suffer these things: nevertheless I am not ashamed: for I know whom I have believed, and am persuaded that he is able to keep that which I have committed unto him against that day. (II Timothy 1:12)*

Yes, we have to suffer sometimes, but in the midst of the suffering, who do we believe? Whose voice are we listening to? God or the enemy? You need to be pursuaded; you must know beyond the shadow of a doubt that God is able to keep what you commit to His care. He only keeps what we commit to Him. If we do not entrust our destiny to Him and let Him guide us, it will never come to pass. **The key to victory is knowing that He is able and has the power and authority to take us out of our mess and into our destiny.**

Let us commit our destiny to Him. Lean on Him, trust in Him, look to Him, follow and listen to Him. Do not listen to the past. Refuse to turn around and go backward, even in your mind. When we make a mistake, we need to confess the sin quickly and ask Him to forgive us and cleanse us from all unrighteousness (I John 1:9). A righteous man will fall seven times, and seven times God will pick him up again (Prov. 24:16). The problem is not that we fall;

it's knowing how to get up when we fall. We will never know success until we understand failure. God doesn't allow us to make it on our own so we can discover that it is *with Christ* that we can do all things. Let us get focused and understand that God has a plan for our life. Let us commit our destiny to Him: our marriage, children, job, our finances and relationships. Don't go by the past anymore. **Submit to God's will and purpose and you will be able to resist the devil, and he will have to flee.** We have to commit to fulfilling God's purpose for our lives. When we do that, God is able to deliver us.

God will bless our mess when we allow Him to! **Often the issues that we have been delivered from and healed of are the very ones God will use to bring healing to others.** There are people in the same place where you were, and they are looking for somebody who made it through. In the midst of our mess, God will bless us and give us the opportunity to be a witness, to bring glory and honor to Him.

> *Blessed be God, even the Father of our Lord Jesus Christ, the Father of mercies, and the God of all comfort; who comforts us in all our tribulation, that we may be able to comfort those who are in any trouble, with the comfort with which we ourselves are comforted by God. (II Corinthians 1:3,4)*

You'll have a testimony, and we overcome the devil by the blood of the Lamb and by the word of our testimony. Our testimony is a powerful tool against the works of the devil.

PROMOTION: COMPLIMENTS OF YOUR ENEMY

It may sound strange, but our enemy serves a very important purpose. He gives us an excuse to be promoted in God. When our enemy comes against us, we need to know that God has great things in store for us. If He didn't have great things in store, the devil wouldn't bother with us. The reason the devil sends all these demon spirits against us is because he hears the sound of thunder and knows something is about to take place in our life. So he sends the demons to stop us, but God will help us throw them off. Satan understands that we have a destiny and he will do anything he can to interfere with it. Actually, the things he tries will only make us stronger and help us to fulfill our call.

Hard and difficult times are a sign that God is getting ready to do something great and the devil is concerned about it. We just need to apply ourselves to the things of God, know that God loves us and that it is His will. When we know someone loves us, we can go the extra mile. He did not put us on this earth to be stuck in a rut. Know that it is God's will to heal us, get us out of the mess and release us into the destiny of our ministry.

The devil does not want us to be free because many others will be set free because of our testimony. Satan can roar, but he cannot bite. We are more than conquerors, not him. Jesus has already made the way to walk out of these things. He has redeemed us by His blood, removed the cloud over our lives, and set our feet upon the solid rock. He gave us our destiny. That is why we are still alive. If there were no hope for us, He would have taken us home to heaven already. **His fingerprints are on us and His destiny is in us.** God chose us in Him before the foundation of the world, and He did not make a mistake. He knew what we would go through; He knew what it would take to get us out of it; and He already paid the price for us to come out... SO LET'S COME OUT!

PRAY THIS PRAYER:

Thank You, Lord, for all that has happened in my life to date. I know that all things work together for good to them that love the Lord and are called according to His purpose. Throughout my difficult experiences, You developed a deeper Christ-likeness in my life that can be used for Your Glory. Help me, Holy Spirit, not to look back and feel sorry for myself but to look forward and know that God will get glory out of my mess. Lord, I believe that You have a great destiny for my life. Thank You for it. Amen.

STUDY QUESTIONS

1. Meditate on Psalm 139:13-17 and Jeremiah 1:4-10, taking a few days to "soak" in each passage.

2. Nothing in our lives ever goes to waste. Think about difficult times in your life and how God could use them to shape your destiny or use you to minister to others. Pray about it and then write the "vision" God gives you.

3. Find a specific scripture in the Bible that you find encouraging at this point in your journey and meditate on it.

CHAPTER SIX
THE FORCE OF FORGIVENESS

Take heed to yourselves: If thy brother trespass against thee, rebuke him; and if he repent, forgive him. And if he trespass against thee seven times in a day, and seven times in a day turn again to thee, saying, I repent; thou shalt forgive him. And the apostles said unto the Lord, Increase our faith. (Luke 17:3-5)

I can imagine the look on the faces of the apostles when Jesus told them they had to forgive to this extent! We already looked at this passage in Chapter Four and concluded that it takes faith in God to be able to forgive like this. Look at how Jesus answered them. It will give us some insight into this problem. The disciples wanted to know how many times they were to forgive someone who offended them over and over.

And the Lord said, If ye had faith as a grain of mustard seed, ye might say unto this sycamine tree, Be thou plucked up by the root, and be thou planted in the sea; and it should obey you. (Luke 17:6)

The Lord said our faith only needs to be the size of a grain of mustard seed. With just a little faith we can speak to this sycamine tree and it will be plucked up. **Unforgiveness is like a sycamine tree whose roots go**

deep inside you and will bring forth criticism, gossip, strife, discord, sickness and disease. It roots itself in your personality, wrapping around your soul like a vine around a tree. Before you know it, it is part of you. You blame others for what happens in your life. You complain. You continually spew out bitterness, strife and discord with your words. But when you choose to release forgiveness, it plucks out the sycamine tree with its deep roots.

The sycamine tree has berries described in the encyclopedia as "blood red" and they leave a stain. Unforgiveness also leaves its stain in us. In the Book of Isaiah, God describes the stain of sin as scarlet (red). He invites us to come and discuss our sins with Him. **He wants to cleanse us from the stain of sin, which includes unforgiveness.**

Come now, and let us reason together, saith the LORD: though your sins be as scarlet, they shall be as white as snow; though they be red like crimson, they shall be as wool. (Isaiah 1:18)

The blood of Jesus takes away the stain of sin and cleanses us white as snow. We want to carry the red mark of His blood, not the red stain of sin!

Whenever we walk by faith and not by sight—not being ruled by our feelings and emotions, but—releasing forgiveness to those who offend us, we start to uproot the sycamine tree in our life. When we forgive, we do spiritual warfare against the enemy. That is because divine forgiveness fires an extremely powerful weapon against satan who's been binding up the other person's mind and ours. The force God releases at that moment is pure power! We don't see it with our natural eye, so we just need to close our eyes and imagine a huge bomb exploding. "I forgive you"—BOOM!

The sycamine tree lodged in our soul will get plucked out and, before we know it, we'll be in our right mind and are delivered. You may truly want to get delivered from the bondage of sin, but if it is just so that you can return to living in sin the way you did before , forget about it. Many Christians want a quick answer to a problem that can only be accomplished through death. That's right, death—as in crucifying yourself. That is the only way to bring deep inner healing. As we crucify our flesh, the inner spirit man in us will be resurrected, whole, delivered and free!

BINDING AND LOOSING

The main theme of Chapter 18 in the Gospel of Matthew is forgiveness. But look at the words of Jesus in verse 18:

Verily I say unto you, whatsoever ye shall bind on earth shall be bound in heaven: and whatsoever ye shall loose on earth shall be loosed in heaven. (Matt. 18:18)

I always wondered why God talks about binding and loosing right in the middle of this chapter about forgiving. It must have something to do with forgiveness. Here's one way I interpret this passage: **When we refuse to forgive, we are bound to the person whom we refuse to forgive. When we forgive them, we are loosed from them.** If you were to physically "hold something against" somebody (a piece of paper pressed against their back, for instance) you would have to stand right next to them all the time and follow them around wherever they go. But when you choose to loose that person (let the piece of paper drop to the ground) you are free to go about your life. They're free and you're free. That's true freedom! Yet, satan does everything he can to resist us. Everything. The devil reads the Word too and he knows the promise in Matthew 18:18:

Verily I say unto you whatsoever you shall bind on earth shall be bound in heaven and whatsoever you shall loose on earth shall be loosed in heaven. (Matt. 18:18)

Hallelujah! Look at the power God gave us. Whatever we bind on earth is bound in heaven. **Notice: Earth moves first and then heaven responds.** Do you see that? What I bind on earth, He binds in heaven.

If I declare it illegal on earth, God says, "Okay, I declare it illegal in heaven." If I take God's Word and declare sickness in my body illegal (bind it up), God says, "I will do the same in heaven." I have to move first because God takes my faith and uses it to bring the things I declare to pass. It takes trust in God's Word to operate in spiritual authority. My faith pleases God, so He responds. **Faith is what moves the hand of God.**

Again I say unto you that if two of you shall agree on earth as touching anything, that they shall ask, it shall be done for them of my Father which is in heaven. (Matt. 18:19)

You and Jesus can agree even if you can't find another person to agree. You can agree with Jesus that, by His stripes, you were healed. Earth must move first, then heaven will move.

First earth, then heaven.

First earth, then heaven.

First earth, then heaven.

Whatever you ask on earth, according to His Word, He will do in heaven. What a wonderful promise! Amen? This is God's power plant.

UNITY IS KEY

One thing we noticed when we moved here to sunny
Florida a few years ago is all the big power plants, and
around each facility is a big fence. You aren't allowed to go
in there unlicensed because you wouldn't know what you
were doing and you might get zapped. You can't get in
unless you have the key to the gate. Well, God has a spiritual power plant, and He has given us the key to get
through the gate. It's here in Matthew 18:15:

> Moreover, if thy brother shall trespass against thee, go and tell
> him his fault between him and thee alone and, if he shall hear thee,
> thou hast gained thy brother. (Matt. 18:15)

Jesus is talking about giving and receiving forgiveness.
He is encouraging us to bring unity and a spirit of oneness
into the Body of Christ. He is commanding us to go out of
our way to restore a brother in Christ. Jesus is telling us
about the awesome force behind forgiveness. Let's look at
verses 21 and 22 again:

> Then came Peter to Him and said, Lord how often shall my broth-
> er sin against me and I forgive him? till seven times? And Jesus
> said unto him, I say not unto thee until seven times but, until sev-
> enty times seven. (Matt. 18:21, 22)

**The key to get through the gate of the power plant is
walking in harmony and forgiveness with one another.** If
you try to go in there as a sinner, the power of God will not
work for you. It will work against you. That's why many of
us have never walked in this great anointing of God. We've
tried to operate His kingdom as a soulish Christian, and it
just doesn't work. We don't see God's power manifest in
our lives. We don't see answers to prayer. We don't see our
faith moving mountains because we haven't gotten hold of
the key to get in.

Of course, the devil does everything he can to keep the key out of your hand. He doesn't want you to get the power, so he'll stir up all sorts of problems and relational issues. He'll try to get you at odds with somebody on the job, at home… and it usually spills over from one person to the next. If you're angry with someone on the job—trust me—you'll blow up at the kids, your husband/wife or both, when you get home. Before you know it, you're upset with everybody and then you'll start living as a recluse. You'll be by yourself because you don't like anybody anymore, including yourself. All this happens because the devil doesn't want you to walk in unity and get into God's power plant.

THE LIFE FORCE OF FORGIVENESS

We want these truths to get deeply ingrained in your spirit. That's why we're bombarding you from all different angles. It must become revelation to you. Forgiveness must become part of your lifestyle. **For some people, this is absolutely a matter of life and death.** They don't see that they're on a collision course with death because their hearts are heavy-laden and their minds are blinded to the truth. The Lord wants to set us free! Every time you flow in forgiveness, God pours out inside you His *zoë*—absolute, everlasting, eternal life—and you get revived, your body gets better equipped to fight off sickness.

> *A merry heart doeth good like a medicine: but a broken spirit dryeth the bones. (Proverbs 17:22)*

A broken spirit dries the bones. Spiritbones, spirit bones. Do you see the connection? What affects our spirit affects our body. The marrow of our bones produces red blood cells and the Bible says that the life is in the blood. So if our bones become "dry" and stop producing the marrow that produces the red blood cells, we will lose much of the force of life. We'll become weak. But a merry heart, a merry spirit, doeth good like a medicine!

When we walk in the Spirit, we cause the power of God's life to flow through us and we continually flow in the supernatural. What is supernatural to us is natural to God. Jesus did miracles all the time because the life of God flowed through Him. When we release the force of forgiveness from inside us, the blood flows and brings life. It brings regeneration. Life is in the blood. Forgiveness is the blood of God. It is the life of God. **The very first thing we receive when we receive His forgiveness is life.**

> *Keep thy heart with all diligence, for out of it are the issues of life.*
> *(Proverbs 4:23)*

Another translation says, "out of it flow the sources of life." Out of our spirit flow the forces of life. When our spirit is filled with forgiveness and we freely give it out to others, there's a force coming in and a force going out. It brings health to our own physical bodies, as well as to the Body of Christ.

Wouldn't it be wonderful if we could still come to church on Sunday, even though we know we blew it, along with everybody else? Wouldn't it be great if, instead of staying home, we came knowing everybody would love us and say things like: "Hey, man, I'm praying for you... Except for the grace of God, I would have done the same thing... I just want you to know I love you... I want you to come here and sit next to me." No judgment. No condemnation.

Wouldn't it be wonderful? Don't you think it would make a difference in the life of the church? "I know you did x, y, and z, but you've repented and I know that God has forgiven you. I forgive you too." Just think about that. If we

81

know we are loved that much, something inside says, "I don't want to do hurtful things to that person anymore." When we are forgiven and they just *keep* forgiving us, something begins to work inside us. It's the Holy Spirit.

However, that's not what we were taught. We were taught that, if we punish somebody enough, treat them rough, retaliate against them enough, then maybe they'll turn around. **Actually, vengeance and retaliation have the exact opposite effect; it drives people away. It is the goodness of God that leads to repentance (Romans 2:4).** It's love that will draw sinners. Can you imagine how packed the churches would be if we expressed divine forgiveness instead of sitting in service, passing judgment on one another! Wouldn't it be wonderful if, by the time we got home, we actually remembered the message instead of having our mind brimming with angry thoughts about each other?

> Beloved, I wish above all things that thou mayest prosper and be in health, even as thy soul prospereth. (III John 2)

The Apostle John, speaking under the inspiration of the Holy Spirit, says "I wish above all things…" He is placing this one thing above your going to church, above your praying, above your ministry work (and these things are important). "I wish above all things that you would prosper and be in good health even as…, even as…, even as…, even as…your soul prospers." As you prosper on the inside, you're going to prosper on the outside and be in good health. Again, here is a direct connection between your inner man/woman and your physical body and your relationships.

WOUNDED SPIRITS

The spirit of a man will sustain his infirmity; but a wounded spirit who can bear? (Proverbs 18:14)

When your spirit is wounded, your body cannot endure or bear up under the weight of infirmity or sickness. In other words, a person with a wounded spirit is more susceptible to sickness and disease.

Many people have come into my (Gaspar's) office over the years for pastoral counseling. They could not sustain their lives: their marriages, their sobriety, their families or their jobs. I would look into their eyes and see that the problem was a wounded spirit. They had nothing left to give them strength. I've heard heart-breaking, horrendous stories. People carry with them for years the terrible hurts and wounds of what other people have done to them. It's only because of the grace of God that I can tell them, "You can forgive." Realistically, I know no human being is capable of forgiving such horrors that have been inflicted on them. God knows that, too. **He doesn't expect us to rely on our own ability to forgive.** It is the power of His forgiveness that He's asking us to use. He gives it to us, so we can then turn around and give it to others. Forgiveness is the foundation of restoration. Without it, we can't get healed.

I (Michele) had a woman say to me one time, "I would rather burn in hell than forgive that person!" I wanted to say to her, "Watch out! You might do just that!" Is it worth it? When we are cool and calm, most of us would agree, no it's not. But when we get caught up in the emotion of the whole thing and carry it around with us every day, it's hard to forgive. It wounds our spirit. God said, "If you don't forgive, I can't forgive you." If we walk according to the flesh and not the Spirit, we allow our spirit to be wounded. That brings death, not life.

The two of us spent several months counseling a woman who had a wounded spirit. We helped her work through the different people in her life that she needed to forgive. She was so wounded that it impacted every aspect of her life. Really, she had no life. Her wounded spirit couldn't sustain her. She was so filled with bitterness that when people saw her coming, they ran the other way. All she did was rehearse over and over what had happened to her in the past. She was consumed. Her only hope was to release all the anger and bitterness she held against people.

It even affected her relationship with God. When we have unforgiveness, how can we have intimacy with God? We can't. So many Christians walk around feeling cold, and they don't even remember the last time they heard from God. They can't get into worship. Do you know what the cause is most of the time? They haven't forgiven the offenses in their lives. It's just not worth it! **God is not asking us to muster it up in our own strength. He says, "I have given it to you freely. Now you pour it out freely on others."**

SELF-FORGIVENESS

There is yet another stumbling block for many of us. We can't seem to receive forgiveness from others. We're sincere when we ask for forgiveness and they're sincere when they give it but, for some reason, when we go to God to confess our sins, something different happens. We can quote I John 1:9, "If we confess our sins, he is faithful and just to forgive our sins, and to cleanse us from all unrighteousness." We believe it with our minds, but not in our hearts. We think *I don't know if I really deserve it,* and we start arguing with God. Of course, we don't deserve it! We can't even earn it! There is nothing good in us. But, praise God, He loves us anyway. Can't we get that right, sooner rather than later?

Can't we realize that if God did not want to forgive us He wouldn't have sent His Son Jesus to make the ultimate sacrifice? We're forgiven! Now let's forgive...starting with ME!

PRAY THIS PRAYER:

Lord, continue to strengthen my born-again spirit with the force of forgiveness. Encourage me not to let my guard down and get caught up in the troubles of life that so often surround me. Help me not to react to those circumstances, but to act Christ-like and be a great testimony of Your power of forgiveness and love. Use me, Lord, to help bring Your kingdom power wherever You send me, especially within my family and friends. With You nothing is impossible. Amen.

STUDY QUESTIONS

1. **Why do you think forgiveness is such a powerful force against the kingdom of darkness?**

2. **Think of anyone who may be holding unforgiveness *toward you* and make plans to put your ministry of reconciliation into action. But don't just plan, ask God to prepare an opportunity for you to go to them and ask forgiveness—regardless of who is right or wrong. Apologize for your part in the offense. The Lord will help you.**

CHAPTER SEVEN
DIE TO YOUR PAST

O bviously satan sees something in us that we do not see in ourselves. We need to grasp the vision that God has for our lives and put the enemy where he belongs—under our feet! First, we need to act on God's Word here on earth and then God will open the heavens and pour out the blessings on us. We need to know *in our hearts* that God loves us, not just in our head. We need to stay in the Word until it comes alive in us. **When there is a Holy Spirit spark between the pages of the Bible and our heart, that's revelation.** We'll know that we know that we know that this is absolute truth. Once we have that assurance, the devil can't steal that Word. Once we really know that God loves us, we can take a licking and keep on ticking. When we don't know it, we back down and give up. That's the difference between revelation knowledge and head knowledge.

> When he was come down from the mountain, great multitudes followed him. And, behold, there came a leper and worshiped him, saying, Lord, if thou wilt, thou canst make me clean. (Matthew 8:1, 2)

Leprosy was the worst of the worst diseases in those days. It was equivalent to AIDS today. People with leprosy were called "unclean"; they were mocked and separated from society and put in leper colonies where no one cared for them. That's exactly where you'd expect to find Jesus. Jesus comes to the worst of the worst. He loves us that much. He leaves the ninety-nine to minister to the one. The leper worshiped Him saying: "I know You can heal me, but is it Your will?"

Jesus said, "I will." God is not a respecter of persons. If He says "I will" to one person, then He'll say "I will" to everybody. It is His will to heal us from hurts and set us free. The problem is not out there. The problem is in us.

FORGIVE AS YOU HAVE BEEN FORGIVEN

One of the hindrances we experience in this forgiveness walk is forgetting how much forgiveness we received from our heavenly Father. Matthew 18:21-35 says,

Then Peter came and said to Him, "Lord, how often shall my brother sin against me and I forgive him? Up to seven times?" Jesus said to him, "I do not say to you, up to seven times, but up to seventy times seven.

For this reason the kingdom of heaven may be compared to a certain king who wished to settle accounts with his slaves. And when he had begun to settle them, there was brought to him one who owed him ten thousand talents. But since he did not have the means to repay, his lord commanded him to be sold, along with his wife and children and all that he had, and repayment to be made.

The slave therefore falling down, prostrated himself before him, saying, 'Have patience with me, and I will repay you everything.' And the lord of the slave felt compassion and released him and forgave him the debt. But that slave went out and found one of his fellow slaves who owed him a hundred denarii's; and he seized him and began to choke him, saying, Pay back what you owe. So his fellow slave fell down and began to entreat him, saying, 'Have patience with me and I will repay you.' He was unwilling however, but went and threw him in prison until he should pay back what was owed.

So when his fellow slaves saw what had happened, they were deeply grieved and came and reported to their lord all that had happened. Then summoning him, his lord said to him, 'You wicked slave, I forgave you all that debt because you entreated me. Should you not also have had mercy on your fellow slave, even as I had mercy on you?' And his lord, moved with anger, handed him over to the torturers until he should repay all that was owed him. So shall My heavenly Father also do to you, if each of you does not forgive his brother from your heart." (Matt. 18:21-35, NAS)

This passage tells us that we will be handed over to the torturers if we do not forgive. Who are these torturers? Have you ever been tormented by physical or emotional pain such as depression, despair or fear every day of your life? These are our torturers. **This is how God will deal with us if we don't forgive.** Notice, at the end of the passage, He adds that we need to forgive *from our heart*. No faking it! God can demand this from us because He knows how much we have been forgiven. The problem is that we forget. We become Christians and we begin to walk in God's grace and to feel good about ourselves in the "religion department", but we forget where we came from.

Hearken to me, ye that follow after righteousness, ye that seek the LORD: look unto the rock whence ye are hewn, and to the hole of the pit whence ye are digged. (Isaiah 51:1)

Did we save ourselves? Did we dig ourselves out of the pit of sin? No, it was God's grace and mercy! But the carnal nature will exalt self, because it is prideful and selfish. We forget how God forgave our offenses to Him when we pour out our judgment and wrath on the people who offend us. Do you think that there is anything that a person on this earth can do to another person that is more serious than what we have done against God? Yet, that is what we are saying when we don't forgive another person and hold their sin against them. So God allows the tormentors to come into our life. That's a principle we need to remember when we're looking for answers to our problems!

> Therefore if thou bring thy gift to the altar, and there rememberest that thy brother hath aught against thee; Leave there thy gift before the altar, and go thy way; first be reconciled to thy brother, and then come and offer thy gift. Agree with thine adversary quickly, whiles thou art in the way with him; lest at any time the adversary deliver thee to the judge, and the judge deliver thee to the officer, and thou be cast into prison. Verily I say unto thee, Thou shalt by no means come out thence, till thou hast paid the uttermost farthing. (Matthew 5:23-26)

God wants us to take the high road in every relationship. Not only do we need to forgive our brother, we need to go to our brother, ask forgiveness and make peace with him so we can live free. We're hit with forgiving from both directions! This forgiveness concept isn't easy, is it? But it is the only way to please the heart of the Father.

SPIRITUAL SMOKE DAMAGE

Many of us are living in the past, so tied to old hurts that we can barely function in the here and now. I (Michele) remember a story my grandmother Mary told me when I was fifteen years old. Her mother-in-law, my great-grandmother, gave all her daughters china as a wedding gift. At my grandmother Mary's wedding, she presented her with a nickel tied up in a handkerchief with about 20 knots in it. She said to Mary, "By the time you finish taking out these knots you'll be too tired to spend that nickel, and you won't waste my son's money." That old wound went very deep. The incident had happened 40 years earlier, but my grandmother related the story to me as vividly as if it happened yesterday.

Getting free from the past is a really BIG issue. **Many of us have been limping through our journey in life, hurt by the negative things done to us or things that we've done to ourselves.** We haven't been able to get over them, so they damage our hearts, our emotions, our thoughts and our feelings. They color the way that we see life, forming a distorted filter through which we look at everything. If you walked into a building with rose-colored sunglasses on and I asked you what color the walls were, you would say "pink." And no matter how many times I told you they are white, we wouldn't see eye-to-eye because you're looking at it through a distorted filter. The hurts and the wounds of the past affect the way we see life in the same way. They affect how we respond to life and they will always be a stumbling block, unless we let God deal with them.

The Lord said in Matthew 5:8,

Blessed are the pure in heart: for they shall see God. (Matt. 5:8)

God wants to purify our heart so we can see Him. He wants to heal us from the damages we have suffered. Sure, some of the damage is as a result of our own wrong decisions because we didn't know Jesus. If you turn the lights off and walk in the pitch-black darkness, you would definitely bump into things and get hurt. That is what life is like without Jesus Christ. We wind up bruised and hurt, dealing with inferiority and rejection.

Then, of course, there are things that people did to us in the past. The devil used them. We are not fighting against

91

flesh and blood, but certainly the devil will use people's words and their hands that were meant to give loving touches to hurt and defile us. We are defiled when someone touches us in an ungodly way and they leave "ungodly fingerprints" on our soul (in our memories and thoughts). Only the blood of Jesus Christ can wash and cleanse us from those thoughts, feelings and emotions. Over time, all these things add up to a wounded spirit.

Whenever we do not forgive, do not walk in the mercy and grace that God has given us—freely we've received, freely we are to give—it turns into a root of bitterness. What's worse, the fire or the smoke damage? If you have ever had a fire or been in a building damaged by fire, you've seen that smoke alone can do as much damage as the actual flames. It's the smoke that kills most people who die in house fires—not the fire itself. Well, **unforgiveness creates smoke damage in our soul and does major injury to the way we think, feel and perceive things.** It distorts our view of God, our life, our destiny and ourselves. We will think everything is okay, when it really is not. Then we constantly blame-shift or play the role of victim, believing that everybody's always picking on us. We buy into the belief that if anything bad is going to happen, it's going to happen to us. This will literally eat us from the inside out.

DON T LET YOUR PAST DICTATE YOUR FUTURE

Even though we have become born again and have a spirit that is brand new, our soul needs to be saved. As we discussed in Chapter Two, salvation is a process. James 1:20 and 21, says,

> *For the wrath of man worketh not the righteousness of God. Wherefore lay apart all filthiness and superfluity of naughtiness,*

and receive with meekness the engrafted word, which is able to save your souls. (James 1:20, 21)

The word "save" here is *sozo* in the original Greek and it means to restore. It's the same meaning as if you took a piece of antique furniture, completely stripped it and gave it a brand new finish. Before you put on the new, you have to strip off the old. God wants to restore our soul by stripping away the filth of a sinful life lived in a fallen world. Our soul is restored when we "receive with meekness the engrafted word". God wants to take the blood of Jesus and wash away all those bad memories and experiences along with the pain, hurt and scars they produced in us, and then impart His vision, His insights and His destiny for our lives. Just like with that treasured antique, soul restoration is a process. It won't happen overnight, but neither will anything go to waste. **Nothing in our life, not even the bad things, are ever wasted.** God uses the things we would have thrown away.

Think about an autumn leaf falling to the ground. It used to be healthy and vibrant, but the seasons changed and the time came for it to let go. So it falls to the ground and starts to nourish the very tree that used to give it life. It even brings forth new life. Our past hurts are alive in us, but God wants us to release them. Nothing that we have gone through goes to waste. It all works together for good to them that love the Lord and are called according to His purpose (Romans 2:28). We might not understand the purpose of our past hurts, but God will use them to bring forth His destiny in our life. It's far from over. The best is yet to come.

GOOD PAIN

James talks about the "engrafted word" which is able to save our souls. To engraft means to plant firmly or establish. Engraft also means to insert a twig or shoot from one plant into a slit made in the bark of another plant. Before you know it, the shoot merges with and becomes part of the original plant. When the bark of the plant is cut, it bleeds sap. The same thing happens when the Word of God is engrafted inside us. It cuts our flesh. It cuts against our old nature and crucifies the carnal part of us. It hurts. But the Word of God is the only road to healing. No one likes to hear that the Word is the only solution because our society wants instant everything, even instant life transformation.

Every time past memories come up along with the opportunity to react in the old way, crucify it and refuse to go in that direction. Don't try to wave a magic wand and hope it will go away like a lot of Christians do. They go to church, get people to lay hands on them and expect a whole lifetime of problems to disappear. It doesn't happen that way. When we get hands laid on us, the change needs to come from the inside so we *see* things differently. Then we can have the discipline to act and react differently. "I found the enemy, and it's me—my flesh." The devil really isn't your major enemy. It's the sinful nature that is lodged within your soul. That's why the Apostle Paul emphasizes to Titus the importance of having a pure heart:

> Unto the pure all things are pure: but unto them that are defiled and unbelieving is nothing pure; but even their mind and conscience is defiled. (Titus 1:15)

In other words, let's get rid of all these bad memories. Don't let the past hinder your destiny. We have a choice to make here: Are we going to build our future on what took place in the past? Or will we overcome the past and let God fulfill the destiny of our lives? It's like trying to sail away on a boat that is anchored to the shore. **When we are embroiled in the past, we can only go so far before we're jerked back into the same old cycle of defeat.**

> *Brethren, I count not myself to have apprehended; but this one thing I do, forgetting those things which are behind. I press toward the mark for the prize of the high calling of God in Christ Jesus". (Philippians 3:13, 14)*

I'm going to say something that may be shocking. God doesn't forget our sins. He doesn't have a bad memory. He *chooses not to remember.* We too must choose not to remember what people did to us and no longer bring it to mind. Choose not to bring up our past failures. Like Paul, we must forget those things which are behind and reach forth to those things which are before us. He calls me more than a conqueror, a child of God, to walk in holiness, receive His glory and have the fulfillment of His promises in my life. If I never let go of it, I will be living in the present but still bound to the past. My destiny will never fully manifest.

When I (Gaspar) got saved, one of the first things I did was quit smoking. In the beginning I was tempted by the smell of smoke. I had a hard time being around smokers. But after a period of time, smoking was a dead issue; it had no life inside me. You could put a pack of cigarettes in front of me or even in my mouth. It didn't make a difference. **As long as the things of the past, the memories, hurts and bruises are living inside us, we will always be an open target for the devil.** As long as there is something inside that is still alive to work with, he will use it. He might use a geographical place, a husband, wife, whatever or whomever he can. It has to be a dead issue inside us for us to resist the temptation outside.

LOCK YOUR WINGS

The Apostle Paul had a guilty past to live down. By his own admission, he was the Church's greatest persecutor, the same Church for which he later laid down his life. He oversaw the stoning of Stephen, the first martyr. By the time, he came to a knowledge of the truth, Paul had a lot to forget. Because he chose to let it go, he was able to go on and write two-thirds of the New Testament.

> If you then be risen with Christ, seek those things which are above, where Christ sitteth on the right hand of God. (Colossians 3:1)

Paul starts off this verse with a question: "*If* you be risen with Christ..." My question to you is, **if we are risen with Christ (born again) don't we have the resurrection power of Christ residing in our spirit to successfully overcome these past hurts?** We will never overcome them as long as we keep talking about them and entertaining the feelings and thoughts. The devil wants to keep us incapacitated by our pain and misery. He wants to blind us to the fact that there's a new world out there, a whole new way of living. He doesn't want us to see the blessing God bought and paid for two thousand years ago. He doesn't mind if we go to church; just don't become the church; just don't walk in the power of Christ. Go ahead and say His name, but just don't understand the power that is in the name of Jesus. Once we do, we become a victor and no longer a victim.

You and I could learn a lot from the eagle. When he sees the storm coming, the eagle locks his wings in an upward position, so the first wind draft takes him straight up until he soars above the storm. The trouble is beneath him. He used those same hurricane winds that could have destroyed him to take him into the heavenlies. We need to lock our affections on the Word of God. Don't be moved by the problems, but let the problems draw us closer to Him. **When we are in Christ, we rise above the circumstances.** So instead of the circumstances moving us, we move our circumstances.

Many of us are on the run. We've run from the first wife; got a second wife; ran from the second wife; and got a third wife. We've run from one job to the next job. We've run from one town to the next town. We're constantly running, constantly moving, and we haven't stood still long enough to see the salvation of the Lord. When someone says something that brings back memories from the past, instead of running, we must stand still and get our mind on the love of Jesus Christ. Release divine forgiveness and let God take us above the storm.

Refuse to bring it up, refuse to talk about it, refuse to allow it to move you. We have to be like the lion trainer who gets that big lion to jump on little boxes and through hoops of fire, and all he has is a whip. Let your spirit man crack the whip and train your soul man. Tell your soul, "This is what we are going to think about. This is what we are going to feel like. This is what we are going to avoid." Give your spirit dominion over your soul. It's a battle and it takes growing up! It takes engrafting the Word of God into your wounded soul until healing takes place.

PUT AWAY CHILDISH THINGS

When I was a child, I spake as a child, I understood as a child, I thought as a child: but when I became a man, I put away childish things. (1 Corinthians 13:11)

Paul must have had today's culture in mind when he wrote this. It really is a battle to take dominion over our soul and be mature men and women of God because of the message we get from our society. We are like Little Johnny sitting in the shopping cart while Mommy shops. He's reaching for cookies, candy and anything else his little hands can reach as they zoom down the grocery aisle. Little Johnny wails and cries, "I want this! I want that!" Instead of spanking him and telling him he's not getting what he wants, Mommy just gives him his way. We have been trained from the time we were little babies to listen to the soul and give it whatever it wants. When we are first born again, we are little children or *brephos* (infant in Greek). But God is raising us up and maturing us. We have to get out of the baby stage and bring "little Johnny" under subjection to our spirit who wants to serve God. We must take the Word of God and discipline our unruly feelings and emotions.

We do not want to hear this because we want the quick solution. "Just wave the magic wand, Preacher. Organize a healing line and lay hands on me." It doesn't work that way. The steps of a righteous man are ordered by the Lord. The steps. It is not an elevator; it is a walk. Each step we take is a decision to go forward and forget those things that are behind us.

THE DEAD DON'T TALK

For you are dead and your life is hid with Christ in God. (Colossians 3: 3)

Those things from the past are dead; we are hidden from them in God. We don't have to listen to them; they no longer have power over us. If we let them have power, they'll lead us into carnality. Babes in Christ are easily drawn back into carnality.

And I, brethren, could not speak unto you as unto spiritual, but as unto carnal, even as unto babes in Christ. I have fed you with milk, and not with meat: for hitherto ye were not able to bear it, neither yet now are ye able. For ye are yet carnal: for whereas there is among you envying, and strife, and divisions, are ye not carnal, and walk as men. (1 Corinthians 3:1-3)

Paul couldn't give them spiritual food because they were living as mere natural men. They were born again, but still acting like baby Christians. You see, babies can't control their emotions. If you put a bunch of babies in a room with one toy, eventually one kid will hit the other kid over the head and they'll all be crying. It's the same in the church. Get together a lot of baby Christians and before you know it somebody's crying, somebody's pouting, and somebody's leaving the church. We are still little babies. Get out of the playpen! Put on your pinstripe suit, grab your briefcase, and do the job that God has called you to do.

Look again at Colossians 3:3-5:

For you are dead, and your life is hid with Christ in God. When Christ, who is our life shall appear, then you shall also appear with Him. Mortify therefore your members which are upon the earth; fornication, uncleanness, inordinate affection, evil concupiscence, and covetousness, which is idolatry. (Colossians 3:3-5)

Since we are dead, since that part no longer has root in us—the part that wants to rise up in retaliation, condemn, judge, and gossip about people; react with hatred and murder—we must crucify them! Mortify those deeds and set your affections on the God of love, whose love never fails. We can't let our past determine our destiny. Die to the craving of the flesh and hide your life with Christ in God. It will happen in due time, in due season, but we have to have the patience of an adult and walk through the process.

PRAY THIS PRAYER:

Thank you, Lord, for healing my heart from past hurts and damaged emotions. You have given me a new beginning. Satan has no power over my life because You are Lord over my thoughts and emotions, and he cannot control me with them any more. Jesus is absolute Lord over my life, and my destiny is under His authority. Like an eagle in the midst of a storm that locks his wings in an upward position and catches the first updraft of the storm's winds, I choose to lock my eyes on my God's promises for me even when it doesn't look like I'm going to overcome the stress that comes in my life. I know I am more than a conqueror in Jesus. Amen.

STUDY QUESTIONS

1. **Write down some examples of "spiritual smoke damage" that may still linger in your life.**

2. **Take the list of people and offenses you made at the end of Chapter 3. Now burn it, bury or flush it so that you can never again retrieve it.**

3. **Now consciously do in your heart what you did symbolically just now, dying to the hurts of your past. See these past hurts as dead, never to be resurrected.**

CHAPTER EIGHT
HINDRANCES TO GETTING FREE

You may have been trying to get free from your past for many years, but I can tell you that there is no magic word or magic wand that will resolve everything in your life. You can't get free with a quick fix. With the help of the Holy Spirit, if you apply yourself, you will be set free from the wounds and damaged emotions you have suffered all these years. Ephesians 1:3 says,

> *Blessed be the God and Father of our Lord Jesus Christ, who hath blessed us with all spiritual blessings in heavenly places in Christ. (Ephesians 1:3)*

God has already blessed us. We are chosen in Him. Get rid of the inferiority complex that the enemy keeps putting on you. Fight against that force that says you are a mess up and that you'll never really be anything special. You are already chosen in Him. You have been chosen to succeed before the foundation of the world. He didn't put you on this earth to fail. He put you here to rule and reign through Jesus Christ and to be successful. He put you here to experience His life and His power. Just because you haven't done it yet, that doesn't mean you won't. God is doing something new in you. Open your eyes to see the new. The Holy Spirit is doing something brand new. You do not have to stay stuck in an eighty-foot hole. He has thrown the Lifeline down to you and His name is Jesus. Just grab on to Jesus and walk the journey. You are set free. If God said it, (and He did!) He will do it if you commit yourself to Him. Scripture after scripture promises us new beginnings, new revelation, new opportunities to do greater things than we did yesterday. God is telling you and me right now, "New things are springing up. Get ready!" We just need to take hold of them and own them.

> *Behold, the former things are come to pass, and new things do I declare: before they spring forth I tell you of them. (Isaiah 42:9)*

> *Thou hast heard, see all this; and will not ye declare it? I have shewed thee new things from this time, even hidden things, and thou didst not know them. (Isaiah 48:6)*

> *Therefore if any man be in Christ, he is a new creature: old things are passed away; behold, all things are become new. (II Corinthians 5:17)*

> *And he that sat upon the throne said, Behold, I make all things new. And he said unto me, Write: for these words are true and faithful. (Revelation 21:5)*

New, new, new! God makes all things new! He wants those old ways, old ideas, and old patterns in our life gone so He can replace them with the new.

> *If the Son therefore shall make you free, ye shall be free indeed. (John 8:36)*

The Son, our Savior, has made us free, so what is our problem? In this chapter we will explore things that hinder us from being free. Too many good people who love Jesus are still in bondage to old ways. I want to see every blood-bought child of God set free from the past!

And ye shall know the truth, and the truth shall make you free. (John 8:32)

Let's get some of His wonderful truths in our spirits!

INNER VOWS

But I say unto you, Swear not at all; neither by heaven; for it is God's throne. (Matthew 5:34)

One powerful tool that the enemy can use against us is inner vows. Inner vows are usually made in our youth and forgotten. Our minds create them, transfer them to our hearts, and our hearts can even transfer them to our bodies. I have prayed for people who, when they were children, made vows that ended up hindering them years later.

One young lady we counseled grew up in a household where her parents fought constantly. There was alcoholism and abuse in the family as well. As a child, she vowed to never get married. She forgot about it, but years later when she wanted to marry, she couldn't. Every time she planned her wedding, it fell through. The Holy Spirit revealed, through prayer, that at one time she had said, "I will never put myself in that kind of position."

I (Michele) made inner vows because of the bad relationship I had with my mother. I didn't realize it until years later when the Holy Spirit brought it to my remembrance. I made those vows because of the great hurt, abuse and pain I suffered as a child. First, I vowed that no one was ever going to hurt me again. Another vow was that no one would ever again tell me what to do. I recalled those vows after I accepted Jesus and wanted to be a submissive wife, but couldn't. There was so much rebellion in my heart I literally *could not* do it. One day while I was praying, by the grace of God, the Holy Spirit took me back to my childhood and I saw myself as that little seven-year-old girl lying in bed crying and saying, "I will never ever let anyone tell me what to do. No one is ever going to hurt me." Praise God! *That* was the answer to why I couldn't submit! When He showed me, I repented of it immediately. In the name of Jesus, I broke the power of those vows over my life.

I know a woman who vowed that she would never have male babies. When she was young, she had to take care of her two-year-old brother. He was miserable. Many years later when she got married, she had a daughter; but her second child was miscarried. Though it was very traumatic, she didn't think much about it. She went on to have a second daughter after that, then miscarried again. It was a boy baby. She ended up having five miscarriages—all male babies. The Lord revealed to her that the problem was an inner vow. It was prayed over, broken and from that point on she had three sons in a row.

Inner vows are literally self–imposed curses. When we say things with our mouth and condemn ourselves or someone else, we often experience the effects of the curse over our lives, without knowing it. We see an example in the Old Testament where an inner vow made by Michal, the daughter of King Saul and wife of King David, actually destroyed her life. Her heart was cold towards God and she mocked her husband David when she saw him rejoicing in the street before the ark of the covenant. She didn't share his zeal for worship or even try to understand it.

And as the ark of the LORD came into the city of David, Michal, Saul's daughter looked through a window, and saw king David leaping and dancing before the LORD; and she despised him in her heart…. Therefore Michal the daughter of Saul had no child unto the day of her death. (II Samuel 6:16, 23)

Because of her hard heart, Michal was deprived of the blessing of having children. Her inner vow caused her to be barren! (I wonder how many people in the Body of Christ are like Michal. When they see someone on fire for God, worshipping with abandon, they mock and despise them, thereby bringing a curse upon themselves.)

PAST MISTAKES

How many times have we been disappointed in ourselves? Maybe we wanted to please other people or even God but fell short, and we can't forgive ourselves. If we disappoint ourselves because we thought we should have done better or disappointed others who thought highly of us—more highly than we thought of ourselves—we can fall into self-rejection and self-condemnation. Go through it a few times and we may develop a poor self-image.

I (Gaspar) remember a young Christian woman who had a conflict in her marriage. She was actually correct in this particular matter, and her husband was wrong. However, he wouldn't own up to his fault and they hurled biting remarks back and forth. Suddenly she stopped and started severely clawing her face. The husband phoned me in a panic because he didn't know what was happening. By the time I got to their home, she was behind the couch with her face marred and bloody. Although this was an extreme reaction, it was deeply rooted in self-rejection. There were things she had never been able to forgive herself of. The devil used this marital conflict to bring self-condemnation.

During another argument she locked herself in a closet. She started out okay but, before long, took all the blame on herself. She saw herself as the victim, the devil got a stronghold in her and she began to self-destruct. In most cases, the hardest thing to do is forgive ourselves. We might not get this extreme, but we may run out, get drunk and try to kill ourselves that way. Or we might hop in the car and drive 100 miles per hour, trying to think of a reason to live.

Left unresolved, past mistakes will have a force in our lives. **Get it into your heart today that you are not perfect and there is no way you can be perfect.** You can even rest in your mistakes because God loves you just the way you are. That doesn't mean that we should repeat our mistakes, but that God unconditionally loves and accepts us, mistakes and all. It is hard for us to understand because we were brought up with conditional love. If you cleaned your bedroom the way you were told, then you were accepted. If you didn't clean it right, you were rejected. Most of us were brought up performance-oriented, and we spend our lives trying to earn people's love.

When we fail, we condemn ourselves. If this cycle continues, we start to view ourselves as a mess up. We may not come out and say these things, but in our mind we shut down. Unforgiveness of self can be a very strong root that produces a poor self-image. We may even develop a fear of failure and become too afraid to try again. But in Jesus Christ, we are more than conquerors.

THE LAW OF JUDGMENT

We can never experience the wonderful liberty that Jesus purchased on Calvary until we stop judging the people who hurt us. Even though it may have happened many years ago, those experiences can still affect us today, and can still open the door for satan to harass us. We can begin to feel we can't even serve God the way we want to. It will hinder our Christian walk. We need to find those roots and ask God to help us get rid of them. Remember what we learned several chapters ago: It's not human forgiveness we need. It's divine forgiveness.

> *Therefore thou art inexcusable, O man, whosoever thou art that judgest: for wherein thou judgest another, thou condemnest thyself, for thou that judgest doest the same things. (Romans 2:1)*

You end up doing the very things for which you judge others. It's a spiritual law and it will come to pass in your life. I (Michele) had an experience years ago that illustrates this point. I shared with you the fact that my mother and I had a bad relationship when I was a child. I judged her and, when I was growing up, I said things like, "I will never treat my husband the way Mom treats Dad.... I will never treat my children that way." The law of judgment is so powerful that when I became an adult, I found myself saying all the same things my mother used to say and doing all the things for which I judged her. It bothered me very much.

Then, years later, God gave me a very special gift that helped me to break free from that bitter root judgment. Near the end of Mom's life, I had the privilege of taking care of her. She had become ill and we took her into our home. One day as I was giving her a bath and washing her hair, I noticed tears coming down her face. I asked her, "What's the matter, Mom? Did I get soap in your eyes?" She looked up at me and said, "No, honey. I just wish that I had been a whole lot more gentle with you." That was my gift from God. At that moment, I released Mom from all the judgments and the unforgiveness from our past together. In that one moment I was set free from the past!

When we judge someone and do not forgive, we hold them to that sin. The scriptures say that whomever you forgive is forgiven and whomever you hold a sin to, it's held to him or her (John 20:23). It keeps that person in bondage.

The Holy Spirit is wonderful. He's our Teacher, our Comforter, and He's the still, small voice of God. As you are reading this, He will bring to your remembrance or reveal to you what some of these hindrances are that cause you to be stuck in the past, unable to get free. These issues make us unproductive and dysfunctional and keep us away from God's best. They make us an open target for the enemy and take us down the wrong road.

FAULTY CONCEPTS ABOUT FORGIVENESS

One faulty, but popular, concept about forgiveness is: *If I forgive, then they'll get away with it.* People will tell you, "Don't let him off the hook. Make him pay!" Even Christians will say this. First of all, don't walk in the counsel of the ungodly, and remember that what you sow is what you wind up reaping.

> *Be ye therefore merciful, as your Father also is merciful. Judge not, and ye shall not be judged: Condemn not, and ye shall not be condemned: Forgive, and ye shall be forgiven: Give, and it shall be given unto you; good measure, pressed down, and shaken together, and running over, shall men give into your bosom. For with the same measure that ye mete withal it shall be measured to you again. (Luke 6:36-38)*

This passage is often used in the context of giving tithes and offerings. A better application concerns showing mercy toward one another. I know I need a lot of mercy in my life. How about you? Well, God says that when we are merciful to others, that is exactly what we will receive in return.

> *For judgment is without mercy to the one who has shown no mercy. Mercy triumphs over judgment. (James 2:13, NKJV)*

We need to let God have His way in people's lives. God is a God of love and that is how He treats people when He brings correction. He loves them into submission. He loved you so much that you were willing to give up your sinful life. Everybody else rejected you, but there was Jesus with His arms open wide. So don't be concerned about the person getting away with their sin. God is a God of love and also justice. How He chooses to deal with the offense is none of your business! You are called to forgive.

Here's another faulty concept about forgiveness: *I will forgive those whom I think deserve it.* God is the only righteous judge. You and I, on the other hand, are unjust. Many times we forgive people if we can get something back from them. It is conditional forgiveness. They bless you, so you let it go. Sometimes we forgive people who are not close to us, but refuse to forgive those who are really close to us. They are the ones we don't want to let off the hook. This attitude that you'll forgive only those who you think deserve forgiveness is totally demonic. Proverbs 14:12 says there is a way that seems right to a man but its end is death. The way that we may think is right is not right. We need to submit ourselves to the counsel of God.

"My unforgiveness will punish them." Have you ever said this? Do you know who gets punished when you do that? You do. You open the door for satan.

> Dearly beloved, avenge not yourselves, but rather give place unto wrath: for it is written, Vengeance is mine; I will repay, saith the Lord. Therefore if thine enemy hunger, feed him; if he thirst, give him drink: for in so doing thou shalt heap coals of fire on his head. (Romans 12:19, 20)

We discussed this in a previous chapter but we believe that it is important enough to look at again. Maybe we didn't get it the first time! Remember that God's wrath is love.

That is how God works. You are not called to avenge yourself; you are called to give God's love and mercy. We can understand the part about feeding our enemy and giving them water, but what about heaping coals of fire on their head? In the Eastern culture of that time, during cold weather, people used to carry a bin of hot coals on their head. (That's how most people from that region carried their load.) Imagine a person carrying the bin of hot coals meeting on the road someone who has offended them. Instead of bypassing or ignoring their enemy, he shares his coals so his enemy too can be warm. That's what we are called to do. Instead of holding things against those who hurt us, we are to share God's love with them. It is an act of love and compassion. Don't be overcome by evil, but overcome evil with good.

> For even hereunto were ye called: because Christ also suffered for us, leaving us an example, that ye should follow his steps. (I Peter 2:21)

Jesus left us an example of how to deal with people who hurt us. So we can follow His role model. Don't forget that when we forgive, it costs something. It will cause us to die to our own feelings and emotions so the love of Christ can flow through us. When people mistreated Jesus, He didn't take revenge on them. When He suffered, He could have called a legion of angels, but He didn't. He committed Himself to God who judges righteously. He let Father God judge the circumstances.

That is what we need to do, because we cannot judge our circumstances from this earthly position. We cannot fairly judge our case from our tainted view. We have to hand the person who hurt us over to God and let God judge him. Say, "Lord, You judge him and I will love him." And how does God judge? He judges them free from sin if that person is a believer in Jesus Christ. And if they are not saved yet, perhaps the love you show them is the exact thing that God wants to use to bring them to salvation! It's a win, win situation! Let God judge because He has a higher vantage point. Do just what He has called you to do, and that is to love.

Here is yet another faulty perception that will hinder our freedom: *I can still treat that person badly even though I have forgiven them.* That is the mindset of the elder son in the story of the prodigal son (Luke 15:11-32). He was bitter because the father loved his younger brother unconditionally. He didn't mind that his brother came back. But to give him the fatted calf, put a robe on his back and a ring on his finger! That made him angry. Like our Father in heaven, the father in the story didn't punish him, but that older brother wanted to make sure that the prodigal was not shown love.

That is where many of us Christians are today. We say we forgive, but we don't want the people to ever forget what they did. We remind them of the incident and we punish them. "You can come back, but I'm not letting you off the hook." That is wrong. That is a carnal attitude. Nail these mindsets to the cross of Calvary! Jesus paid the price for your freedom and theirs. Remember, "Whom the Son sets free is FREE INDEED!"

PRAY THIS PRAYER:

Thank You, Lord, for setting me free from those things that have held me back from serving You and reaching my God-given destiny. Whom the Son sets free is free indeed, and in Jesus I am free and choose to stay free with the help of the Holy Spirit. In Jesus Christ, I am more than a conqueror and refuse to allow the devil to keep me in the bondage of unforgiveness anymore. Amen.

STUDY QUESTIONS

1. Have you in the past held any of the faulty concepts about forgiveness mentioned here? If so, how has your mind changed now that you've read this chapter?

2. What are some hindrances to getting free that you see in your own life (i.e. inner vows, judgment, past mistakes)?

3. Write out in your own words what this scripture means:

   For to him who has shown no mercy the judgment will be merciless, but mercy [full of glad confidence] exults victoriously over judgment. (James 2:3, Amp.)

CHAPTER NINE
ROOTS PRODUCE FRUITS

In the book of Hosea, God tells the people that they are destroyed for lack of knowledge. They rejected His wisdom and counsel. God forbid we reject His knowledge! No, we need to be people who seek after divine revelation and wisdom. We can't be ignorant and leave ourselves open to the wiles of the enemy. You and I need to understand the roots of the issues in our lives. *Why is this happening to me? Why am I sick all the time? Where is this depression coming from?* Every fruit has a root. We need to discern God's wisdom to know the answers to these questions.

> *If any of you lack wisdom, let him ask of God, that giveth to all men liberally, and upbraideth not; and it shall be given him. (James 1:5)*

People come to church and the Word goes in one ear and out the other. They don't let it take root and give rise to the desire to crucify their flesh. **There has to be death before there can be resurrection.** There are no short cuts. The Holy Spirit will help you to identify the roots to these hurts, wounds and bruises in your life. Maybe it started in your mother's womb. It could be a bloodline carried down from generation to generation. Then the devil adds to it by placing an assignment over your life. Repeatedly you find the same issues arising again and again because you deal with the symptoms of the problem, but never the cause. We pluck off the fruit without digging out the root.

We can tell what is inside by the words we speak. We can either speak out of our spirit or from our soul. Unfortunately, sometimes we do both. When we come to church we say "hallelujah" and "glory to God." At that point we are speaking from our spirit. Other times we are home yelling and screaming and cursing, speaking out of our soul. Yes, we are saved. Our spirit is born again, but our soul needs to be restored.

We have to say, "Lord, I choose to allow You to heal my life. I desire that You show me the roots to all the problems I am dealing with." We have to walk the journey. It's not going to just happen. God doesn't do anything beyond our free will. He gave us the power of choice. We can choose not to harbor hatred, jealousy and bitterness in our heart because that root of unforgiveness that was inside of us is no longer alive. It's dead. Get it out, rip it up. It doesn't have the right to have roots in us anymore because we are born again.

THE POWER OF AGREEMENT

We have a prayer counseling ministry in our church, and one thing the Pastors do in the pre-counseling is identify the roots of problems, which an assigned prayer team then prays for. We ask diagnostic questions that will help us identify the root of the problem that is bearing fruit in a person's life. The person often can't see it on their own. We need each other. God made us that way.

Two are better than one; because they have a good reward for their labour. For if they fall, the one will lift up his fellow: but woe to him that is alone when he falleth; for he hath not another to help him up. Again, if two lie together, then they have heat: but how can one be warm alone? And if one prevail against him, two shall withstand him; and a threefold cord is not quickly broken. (Ecclesiastes 4:9-12)

When two or three are gathered together in His name He says, "I am in your midst." He made us people of relationship. That is why satan doesn't want us on good terms with each other. He knows there is power in relationships that goes beyond the natural realm that will deliver us and set us free. When God is for us who can defeat us?

For the LORD shall comfort Zion: he will comfort all her waste places; and he will make her wilderness like Eden, and her desert like the garden of the LORD; joy and gladness shall be found therein, thanksgiving, and the voice of melody. (Isaiah 51:3)

It is God's desire and express purpose to impart healing and comfort to those wounded areas. Let's say we have a deep cut. Proper healing takes place from the inside out. If the wound only healed superficially, it would still be very sore as the skin grew over it. If you were to bump into something, it would still be tender and you would feel pain. To the natural eye, it would look okay, but there's still a wound under there. (In fact, an unhealed wound like this can eventually get infected; start smelling and can even lead to gangrene!)

That is exactly what happens to us. Outwardly, we look all right. We smile and say everything is fine, but when we get around certain people who say certain things to us or we are in a certain tight situation, it triggers pain! And because it hurts us, we react in a way that is outside the will of God. It triggers a deep visceral reaction from us that we don't even understand. We are hurt and it's still affecting us. The devil begins to dictate our steps rather than God. We need to let the Lord bring us to the place where we can cut these things at the roots.

We are not fighting against flesh and blood. People are not our problem. Ephesians 6 tells us that we are fighting against the wiles (or methods) of the devil. He has a strategy to make us stumble and hinder us from getting to the next blessing. Just when we seem to get there, we have a breakdown. (Hallelujah Breakdown). Just when we are ready to get over, BAM! Everything gets knocked out from underneath us. Eventually, we just want to give up. Then the devil mocks us and says, "Aha! I got you." But, let's look at what God has to say in the book of Ezekiel about the enemy who says, "Aha!"

> Son of man, because that Tyrus hath said against Jerusalem, Aha, she is broken that was the gates of the people: she is turned unto me: I shall be replenished, now she is laid waste: Therefore thus saith the Lord GOD; Behold, I am against thee, O Tyrus, and will cause many nations to come up against thee, as the sea causeth his waves to come up. (Ezekiel 26:2, 3)

The Lord says that He is destroying the enemy, the one who taunts you with failure and defeat. God will meet us in the midst of our life's deepest hurt. He is there all the time. We can often be like the disciples who did not recognize Jesus when they were on the boat during the storm. Many times we do not recognize Him either because we are not looking for Him.

BLOODLINES

There really is a root to every hurt and bad memory that we deal with today. And we are not just fighting our own demons; we are also fighting our parent's devils. The same

116

events that took place in our family in previous generations are unfolding in *our* life today. If we think about it, the things we deal with now are probably not new. We need to discover what demon spirits harassed our father, our father's father and our grandfather's father so we can apply the blood of Jesus Christ to the roots. Determine what curses have been passed down to you because of sins they committed. They have been passed down, whether we like it or not. God never intended it to be that way. He intended that His nature would be the one passed down. That is why, when Adam fell, it was so devastating. It meant that all mankind would now be birthed with the nature of sin, rather than the nature of God.

The devil has assigned familiar spirits to our family and that is what we are dealing with. A familiar spirit is assigned to the bloodlines that run through families. They will cause the habit pattern of a particular sin to continue through the generations. That explains why we find that some families are into gambling; some are into drinking; some are plagued by divorce; others are continually overrun with rage and bitterness. Each family seems to have a little different corner of the market on sin. Not everybody is the same. Yes, sin is sin, but people's personalities and identities are different. We can follow our identity in our family bloodline going back from generation to generation. We need to know the root of our sin. Once we find the root we can then do away with the force of temptation that is coming against us all the time. It does not change the fact that we still have to crucify that flesh, but there is a root. There is a root to the fruit.

We can be affected by what our father and grandfathers have done in their lives. We can be affected in a good way and we certainly can be affected in a bad way. The root of unforgiveness can already have taken hold of us from our father's loins as the seed in our mother's womb. We carry that nature inside of us. The iniquity (or power) behind the sin is passed down to the child from the father. It is true that we are born again, old things are passed away and behold all things have become new. (But as I have emphasized several times, this is referring to our spirit.) This iniquity lodges itself in the soul and can make us prone to walk in unforgiveness. For some people, it just seems to be a vein in their family and if you look back in the history of their family you will find that it was in their father and grandfather as well.

> *And the LORD passed by before him, and proclaimed, The LORD, The LORD God, merciful and gracious, longsuffering, and abundant in goodness and truth, Keeping mercy for thousands, forgiving iniquity and transgression and sin, and that will by no means clear the guilty; visiting the iniquity of the fathers upon the children, and upon the children's children, unto the third and to the fourth generation. (Exodus 34:6-7)*

> *Our fathers have sinned, [and are] not; and we have borne their iniquities. (Lamentations 5:7)*

MOTHER'S WOMB

Another area we need to gain knowledge about are the root issues that come from our mother's womb. Many things happen to us in our mother's womb. We mistakenly believe that we were oblivious before we were actually born. The fact is we were already a complete spirit and soul while our body was being formed. We always existed in the heart of God. He told Jeremiah that He knew him even before he was in his mother's womb. Even before you were a seed in your mother's womb God knew you. You came from the heart of God. You are not just a happenstance. He pre-determined and pre-destined that you be here on this earth. Isn't that wonderful? You are not just an "Oops!" or a bleep on a monitor, or a mistake on a night when there was nothing else to do! God preplanned you even before you were in your mother's womb. But while you were in the womb things were taking place.

The devil hates the seed the woman carries and he will do everything to destroy her. This pattern began at the fall of man in the Garden.

> *And I will put enmity between thee and the woman, and between thy seed and her seed; it shall bruise thy head, and thou shalt bruise his heel. (Genesis 3:15)*

Of course the seed here ultimately means the Messiah, Jesus. But the enmity is also against the woman. God created woman as a force to be reckoned with and the devil knows it. So he marks her as a number one target, especially when she is carrying a baby. **Pregnant women need to speak life over the child in their womb and release good things into their life.** Expectant mothers, if you are going through some issues, be careful not to transfer your feelings to your baby. It will affect and mark your child.

> *Yea, thou heardest not; yea, thou knewest not; yea, from that time that thine ear was not opened: for I knew that thou wouldest deal very treacherously, and wast called a transgressor from the womb. (Isaiah 48:8)*

Isaiah says something went wrong while this child was still in the mother's womb that caused him to come out as a transgressor—to be literally wicked. Things may have happened in our mother's womb, especially in the area of unforgiveness, hatred and bitterness. If a mother had a husband who left or abused her, or if there were major fights this gets transferred to the child. As our body was being developed our spirit and soul were aware of their environment and received and absorbed things.

We are not making this up. A study was done showing that children in the mother's womb can recognize the father's voice. When they are born, they respond more to the father's voice than all the voices around them. Today there are technological advancements in sonograms. They can film the facial expressions of a baby in the womb. They see that even in fairly early stages of development the child can show emotions. There is a film that was made by a right-to-life group that is particularly chilling. It shows the baby actually pushing away from the abortionist's suction tube, trying to avoid it, trying to cling to life. We hear stories of people who said that their mother tried to abort them but they survived. I am sure that they have suffered some effects from that terrible experience.

Find out if your mother was going through some things while she was carrying you. Were some issues carried down? Was she going through a hard time in her marriage? If you are angry toward men or have an attitude of unforgiveness to authority figures, is it possible that your mother went through things like that? When you were younger, is it possible that she talked to you about it? Or maybe your father was always blaming your mother for things.

Behold, I was shapen in iniquity; and in sin did my mother conceive me. (Psalm 51:5)

David talks about how he was formed and shaped and mentions the possible root of his problem. He said that while he was in his mother's womb, he was being formed in iniquity. In other passages we can read between the lines and gain insight to his background and what he went through as a child. Was he born in sin? Was he the product of an adulterous affair? It's possible. According to historians David was the only one of his brothers who had red hair. He was the youngest child yet he was the one who was sent out to watch the flock in dangerous places while his older brothers were home. He mentions that as a young shepherd he had to fight against the lion and the bear. This does not sound like such a healthy childhood.

Is it possible that his family rejected him because he was different? The Prophet Samuel was sent to David's house to anoint the new king of Israel, chosen by God to replace King Saul. David's father brought all of his sons out to be introduced to Samuel. When God told Samuel that none of these men were His choice, he asked Jesse if he had any other sons. It was only then that he said he had one more son and sent to the field to get David. It seems like David's family did not value him. Why?

MULTIPLIED CURSES

David himself reveals that iniquity was passed down to him from his father while he was in his mother's womb. He then passed those same bloodlines down to his children—except multiplied. David had children who were filled with lust, who committed murder and who raped and abused each other and turned against him. Second Samuel Chapter 13 talks about the life of Amnon, one of King David's sons. When a bloodline becomes a root, it is not carried down in the same measure as our father's. It actually gets multiplied thirty-, sixty- and a hundredfold. David was filled with lust. As a result, David's son Amnon was filled with lust. The Bible tells us that when the kings went out to battle, David stayed home. One evening he was spying on Bathsheba while she was bathing. Lust was an issue for him, or he would have turned away. So he sends for Bathsheba, commits adultery with her, impregnates her and kills her husband to hide his sin. As mentioned previously, David himself may have been the result of an adulterous affair. Now an adult, he is a King, he loves God, but he is not perfect. God calls him "a man after My own heart". AFTER. Not that he was like God, but that he was striving after God the Father to worship and love Him. God honored that despite all of his faults. However, David paid a dear price because his sin carried down to his sons.

Amnon schemed and then raped his own half-sister Tamar because he lusted after her. Tamar's life was destroyed. She became a victim of the bloodline curse. When bloodlines get passed down, the offspring become perpetrators and as well as victims. You might not be the one who sins in your bloodline, but you could wind up receiving the result of the sin.

But when King David heard of all these things, he was very wroth. (II Samuel 13:21)

David was angry, but the Bible never mentions that he brought correction or punishment to Amnon. Amnon went about his business as the King's son. Absalom, another of King David's son, was totally outraged by his father's failure to discipline his brother. Because David did not react the way Absalom thought he should have, he judged his father.

How many times have we been angry and unforgiving to someone who didn't bring justice the way we thought they should have? How many times have we drawn conclusions and passed judgments against people because they didn't do what we thought they should have? How many times have we been angry with God because He didn't resolve an issue in the way we thought He should have? Maybe we said "Why didn't You heal and deliver this person?" or "Why didn't You bring the finances that I needed?" and so on.

Parents have to be careful that they do not provoke their children to wrath. Ephesians 6:4 says, "Father's provoke not your children to wrath." Parents should not favor one child over another or tempt a child to take matters into their own hands by failing to bring needed correction to a sibling. This will provoke them to anger, bring roots of bitterness and set them up to go through life with the same seed as their parents. We want our children to respect authority so they will succeed.

After two full years, Absalom takes matters into his own hands and plots to have his brother killed. He feels that it has been long enough. He is angry with David and Amnon and he can not forgive them so he has Amnon killed. When David hears about it he is deeply wounded. If David had true understanding of bloodlines, he would have seen that the murder his son committed was a result of the bloodline. To cover the sin of adultery with Bathsheba, David had her husband murdered, so now we see his son is also committing the same sin even though it is for a different reason. His son murdered because of unforgiveness and revenge.

Unforgiveness left in our heart will eventually turn to murder. We kill people over and over in our mind and with our words, and eventually for some people they can wind up committing actual murder. Years ago there was a case in the news about the Menendez brothers who were abused by their parents for years. They had so much bitterness in their hearts that they schemed to kill their parents. They had already murdered them in their hearts long before they actually murdered them in reality. Unforgiveness turned into a root of bitterness can easily turn into murder.

UNFORGIVENESS LEADS TO BETRAYAL

Absalom said moreover, Oh, that I were made judge in the land, that every man which hath any suit or cause might come unto me, and I would do him justice! (II Samuel 15:4)

After Absalom kills Amnon, he later betrays his father David, tries to take his throne and is killed in the process. A traitor's end is death. **Betrayal, a companion of bitterness, starts with unforgiveness.** We see the devastating effect of the sinful bloodline in Absalom's life because he ends up being killed. It was very tragic for King David!

Judas is, of course, the Bible's most infamous betrayer, and he was chosen by Jesus. Why did Judas betray Jesus? He really did not respect Him and had no concept of what God was doing through Jesus Christ. He felt that Jesus was "misspending" the money. How? Jesus was giving money to the poor and Judas wanted it in the treasury so he could steal from it. He was angry with Jesus and judged Him because He walked in mercy. He judged Jesus, held unforgiveness toward Him and eventually he betrayed Him. When all was said and done, Judas hanged himself.

When we expect someone to act on our behalf or benefit us in some way and they fail to meet our expectations, we can get offended, make judgments and unforgiveness can take hold of our heart. If not dealt with, it grows into a root of bitterness and we become betrayers, just like Absalom and Judas. These spiritual laws have authority over our lives and affect us, but the blood of Jesus Christ sets us free from that. If you identify that there is a root of unforgiveness in your heritage, apply the Blood of Jesus Christ to your bloodline, cancel it and be delivered from the demon spirit that works legally through the natural and spiritual bloodline. Great deliverance comes when we break a bloodline over our life. The demon assigned by satan through the bloodline will now become illegal and will lose its authority and influence. If there is legal ground, he will stay and work and test and tempt you all the time. I agree that you have been "legally" set free through the blood of Jesus Christ, but in some areas you have not "experientially" been set free. Experientially, means you have applied what God has done for you to your life and are now walking in the manifestation of it. You can talk about something, but unless you experience it, until you see the fruit, it's just head knowledge, a theory. We want to experience it. Amen?

GUARD YOUR HEART

Blessed are the pure in heart: for they shall see God. (Matt. 5:8)

Jesus says the pure in heart are blessed for they shall see God. This Word "heart" is not referring to the physical organ, but to our spirit. When we become born again, our spirit becomes brand new. It is like pure, clear water; but sin taints it. When we pour dirt into this crystal clear water, it becomes cloudy. Sin distorts our heart and we are no longer able to see God or experience Him the way we should. And, of course, the more we sin, the more wounded our spirit becomes. No wonder we can't hear God. Now, before we were saved and our spirit was filled with sin there was nothing we could do to make it right. We couldn't save ourselves. We couldn't purify our old nature. We needed a Savior.

Salvation is a gift from God, and He doesn't repent of His gifts. But the devil is trying to do everything he can to get rid of the power source in our life. Our heart is the very foundation of the power of God. When we forgive, we release a powerful force that will tear down every stronghold of satan. The devil does not want us to get serious with this thing. He does not want us to start loving our neighbor. He does not want us to submit to those in authority in the body of Christ. He does not want us to strive for unity, because he knows that when we do, there is going to be a great release of God's power. He can not stop it after it is released because life always overcomes death. Light always destroys darkness. Good always overcomes evil, and love always defeats hate. God tells us to watch our heart with all diligence. When we are walking in forgiveness, our spirit is going to get fat. It is the only place we can get obese and it's okay. It is all right to have a big, fat spirit. As our spirit goes, so goes our body (not the fat part!) As our spirit goes, so go our relationships.

When we are not forgiving, we walk through life wounded. We find ourselves saying things we would not normally say as a Christian. We find ourselves backsliding, going backwards instead of going forwards.

For if you forgive men their trespasses, your heavenly Father will forgive you. (Matthew 6:12)

There is a condition, a spiritual law. If we forgive, then He will forgive. If we do not forgive, then He has to hold back forgiveness. Sin separates us from God. It is not that He wants to push us away, but our sins separated us. Our disobedience has caused God's face to turn from us and He will let us have our own way. We do not want to be on our own without God. So if you started off your Christian life on fire for Jesus, wouldn't miss a service, gave tithes and offerings and you had a strong desire to please God; but now two or three years later, you don't attend church regularly, you don't care about tithes and offerings and you don't read your Bible, then it's a clear sign that you are in a backslidden condition. **More than likely it is because of unforgiveness.** Its effects are truly devastating.

SICKNESS AND DISEASE

This is a big issue. Unforgiveness makes you an open target for the devil to bring disease knocking at your door. Doctors today agree with what the Bible said thousands of years ago. Most sickness and disease is rooted in our emotions and attitudes (our heart condition.) Most people are so hardhearted that they do not recognize it, but it is true. You can see the fruit in the way they talk, walk and live. Even Christians can be filled with the poison of unforgiveness. Of course, on Sunday we hear them shouting, "Hallelujah, glory to God, praise the Lord, thank you Jesus, I am bringing my tithes up to the altar!" But the course of their life has been a pattern of human forgiveness (unforgiveness) and it drains their source of life and health. Their spirit, their very heart is wounded.

We quoted this scripture earlier, but it bears repeating.

Keep thy heart with all diligence, for out of it are the issues of life (Proverbs 4: 23)

Another translation says, "out of it flow the sources of life." God tells us to *keep* our heart. To *keep* actually means to guard. God says that we should not only guard our heart, but that we must guard it diligently! Why? Because the sources of our life flow out of our heart. If we do not guard our heart and we let unforgiveness, bitterness or any other manifestation of sin come into our heart, then there will be a different flow. It certainly will not be a flow that brings life to us. The Bible says that out of the abundance of the heart the mouth speaks. So if we want to learn what is in our heart, all we need to do is listen to the words that we speak. Are we speaking words of life, or words of death?

But the tongue can no man tame; it is an unruly evil, full of deadly poison. Therewith bless we God, even the Father; and therewith curse we men, which are made after the similitude of God. Out of the same mouth proceedeth blessing and cursing. My brethren, these things ought not so to be. Doth a fountain send forth at the same place sweet water and bitter? (James 3:8-11)

This is very interesting. We bless God with our words, but we are also responsible for what we speak to each other. If our words are bitter, not sweet, it means that we are not diligently guarding our heart. One of the main sources of bitterness is unforgiveness. **I believe that the bitterness so many of us live with deep inside wounds our spirit and poisons our bodies with disease.** I pray that we will gain understanding of this and learn how to release a sweet flow of life out of our heart!

So Moses brought Israel from the Red sea, and they went out into the wilderness of Shur; and they went three days in the wilderness, and found no water. And when they came to Marah, they could not drink of the waters of Marah, for they were bitter: therefore the name of it was called Marah.

And the people murmured against Moses, saying, What shall we drink? And he cried unto the LORD; and the LORD shewed him a tree, which when he had cast into the waters, the waters were made sweet: there he made for them a statute and an ordinance, and there he proved them. (Exodus 15:22-25)

The people came to bitter waters and they had nothing to drink because the waters at Marah would make them sick. Only God could take the bitterness and make it sweet. How did He do it? He provided a tree that turned the water sweet when Moses cast it into it. What is the tree He provided for us? It is the cross of Calvary. So many of us have repeatedly swallowed "marah" (bitterness). We haven't gone to the Lord with it because we think that it is just part of life. We are murmuring and complaining like the Children of Israel. They had just left the Red Sea where God had delivered them in a spectacular way. Yet they complained because of lack of faith. Aren't we like that? We forget all the wonderful things God did for us and we complain and become bitter with life, spewing out bitter waters from our hearts. There is only one way to remove the bitterness! God says, "Come to Me. I have the answer. I have the tree. I have Calvary. I can give you sweet waters that will bring you life and health!"

HEALED OR MADE WHOLE?

In the Gospel of John we see a paralytic man by the pool of Bethesda who had an encounter with Jesus. There are several interesting points here to look at.

> *And a certain man was there, which had an infirmity thirty and eight years. When Jesus saw him lie, and knew that he had been now a long time[in that case, he saith unto him, Wilt thou be made whole? (John 5:5, 6)*

The impotent man answered him, "Sir, I have no man, when the water is troubled, to put me into the pool: but while I am coming, another steppeth down before me." (The man did not answer the question. He did not say that he wanted to be made whole; he just complained to Jesus and blamed his circumstances on others. He sounds bitter. I think he was just resigned to the fact that this was his lot in life.)

> *Jesus saith unto him, Rise, take up thy bed, and walk. And immediately the man was made whole, and took up his bed, and walked: and on the same day was the sabbath....*

> *Afterward Jesus findeth him in the temple, and said unto him, Behold, thou art made whole: sin no more, lest a worse thing come unto thee. (John 5:8, 9, 14)*

Jesus connected the sin in the man's life to his sickness. Not only was he paralyzed, but he was angry and unforgiv-

129

ing. You can hear it in his words. Jesus told the man to rise, pick up his bed and walk. Jesus is also telling us to rise, to pick up the bed of bitterness we have made to lie down on and to walk! He is telling us that we too are to sin no more lest a worse thing come upon us! It is more than just being healed. It is about being made whole!

Why is it important that we avoid sin and keep our spirit whole? Because, as we saw in Proverbs 4:23, the forces of life flow from our spirit. God heals us from the inside out. Some people get healed on a prayer line, but find that they get sick again. There's a reason for that.

> *When the unclean spirit is gone out of a man, he walketh through dry places, seeking rest; and finding none, he saith, I will return unto my house whence I came out. And when he cometh, he findeth it swept and garnished. Then goeth he, and taketh to him seven other spirits more wicked than himself; and they enter in, and dwell there: and the last state of that man is worse than the first. (Luke 11:24-26)*

According to what Jesus is telling us, even when someone is healed and a spirit (in this case, the spirit of infirmity) has been cast out, they may end up even worse than they began. How does that happen? They were never made whole and their spirit wasn't able to sustain them. This explains why we see people falling and backsliding after the music stops and after the prayer line ends. They are healed, but because their spirit is not whole, it is not able to maintain the healing.

If our spirit is cloudy, filled with bitterness and defiled by sin, it is going to hinder the healing process. Ask the Holy Spirit to show you any hidden sin—especially unforgiveness. Even if you have forgiven, it could be you have walked in just human forgiveness, not divine forgiveness. Ask God to make you whole...spirit, soul and body. Throw the tree of Calvary into your bitter waters and watch them become sweet again!

TORMENTING SPIRITS

We looked at Matthew 18:23-35 in a previous chapter. This is a parable that Jesus tells about a man who owed a lot of money to his master. He was shown mercy and did not have to pay back his debt. Unfortunately he did not show the same forgiveness to someone else who owed him just a small amount of money. He sent him to jail. (Just like we do to the people we lock up in the prison of unforgiveness.) When the master heard about it he was angry and handed him over to tormentors. We need to pay close attention to what Jesus is really saying here because so many of us are tormented by our emotions. We are robbed from experiencing the joy of the Lord, which gives us strength (Nehemiah 8:10).

I believe we need to really cleanse our hearts and purge the unforgiveness we have toward one another and not allow offenses to rule our lives. **We do not want to be handed over to our enemy to be tormented!** His master called the man who refused to forgive, a wicked servant. If we don't forgive or give only human forgiveness, we are wicked. It is evidence our heart is defiled and we are not walking according to the Spirit of God. The law of the Spirit of life in Christ Jesus has set us free from the law of sin and death. The Law of Christ is the law of love. God considers it wickedness when we don't forgive.

Years ago, there was a woman in our congregation who was terribly tormented with fear. It really took a strong hold of her and finally opened the door to a *spirit of fear*. When a demon spirit comes, often the problem didn't start off as spiritual. It usually starts with emotions that are controlled

131

by circumstances instead of by God. If our emotions are under the control of our flesh rather than the Spirit of God, it will open the door for a demon spirit to come in. That is what happened to this woman who was tormented by fear. She was afraid to leave the house; she wouldn't go out of her front door. She was afraid, but she didn't know what she was afraid of. If she drove her car, she would feel like throwing herself out of the car while it was moving. It was terrible for her to be held in captivity by such limitations.

We were asked to visit and pray for her. As we interviewed her, we found that she had an incredible amount of unforgiveness towards her husband. She had a bad marriage and her children took the husband's side and turned against her. She was wrongfully accused of things she hadn't done and was bitter as a result of this. She was so bitter that she refused to forgive. Fear controlled her to the extent that she couldn't even go shopping. She was afraid of crowds. On our first visit we prayed for her and put her in our car. She was in the front seat in the middle (between the two of us), because we knew she would try to throw herself out of the car. We prayed for her as we drove, then came home and prayed more. After a few weeks, she got delivered. But the key to her healing was receiving God's forgiveness in her own life and then she was able to release it to her family.

A spirit of torment can also come in the form of negative thoughts continually bombarding us, wicked imaginations, self-condemnation and self-rejection. Many people are overwhelmed with these things. You see them in hospitals calling out the names of people they knew long ago. I personally believe that Alzheimer's can be rooted in unforgiveness and roots of bitterness. It has been around for years and no one knows what causes it. But you will find bitter people in nursing homes, yelling at a son, father, or mother who has passed away years ago.

LUST AND PERVERSION

Lust and perversion can also be connected to unforgiveness. When a man has been manipulated and controlled by a mother, or a female authority in his life, he often winds up marrying someone equally dominating. He might be steeped in pornography, sexual lust and unforgiveness towards women that can be traced back to his relationship with his mother. Retaliation, control, manipulation and a "user" mentality begin to open the door for lust and perversion. This is not the only reason, but it is one of the reasons for struggles with lust.

You might be dealing with pornography or lustful thoughts that no one really knows about. You might be connected to pornographic web sites or Playboy magazines etc, and doing these things in secret. You are a Christian and don't know why you are still bound up. Yes, it could be a bloodline, but it also might be a true root of bitterness towards a mother or a wife or a woman who played an important part in your life. Ask the Holy Spirit and He will reveal it to you.

So once again we see that unforgiveness is a major weapon the devil uses against us. He has been found out! Every time we operate in unforgiveness; sickness overshadows our spirit, makes our heart bitter and saps us of strength. We do not need to wonder anymore why our mind is not right, our bodies are not healthy, and our relationships are going astray. There will be fewer trips to the Doctor's office and Psychiatrist's couches when the body of Christ finally makes the connection between forgiveness and our physical and emotional health.

PRAY THIS PRAYER:

Dear Lord, You have delivered me from the roots of destruction in my life by the blood of Jesus. I no longer have to fear my past because You have set me free through Jesus Christ, my Lord and Savior. I choose to guard my spirit by walking the love walk in Jesus and allowing the Holy Spirit to flow forgiveness through me every day. Now the Blood of Jesus flows through my veins and I am truly a new person in Christ. I declare that only the fruits of peace, joy and forgiveness are manifested in my life and I am a blessing to everybody that the Lord brings into my life. I no longer live under a curse but under a blessing for the rest of my life in Jesus. Amen.

STUDY QUESTIONS

1. Ask the Holy Spirit to show you any hidden sin that could hinder your healing. Once He shows you, confess it and ask God to forgive you and heal you in that area.

2. Now ask the Holy Spirit to show you any bloodline curses that may have been passed down to you. If possible, get someone to help you pray to break them over your life.

CHAPTER TEN
ANGER: THE COUNTERFEIT PASSION

A nger is a very strong emotion! We have all witnessed the destruction it can bring to our lives and to the people around us. We pray that the Holy Spirit will use this chapter to impart revelation, understanding and healing to this misunderstood part of mankind's nature, so you can be free from its bondage.

Emotions are a gift from God. Our ability to express, be aware of and process our emotions sets us apart from the rest of creation. It is true that many of God's creatures can show fear, sadness and anger. But only man can consciously express emotions; only man can shed tears. Unfortunately, the church today makes it seem that feelings and emotions are bad. That is not true. There are a range of emotions that God expresses. He is described in the Bible as feeling jealous, sad, joyful, and zealous. The Holy Spirit can be grieved. The Gospels tell us that Jesus felt love, anger, indignation, distress, sorrow, surprise, agony, joy, and compassion. He even wept at the tomb of Lazarus.

The writer of Hebrews tells us that the range of emotions that mankind experiences were also experienced by

Jesus Christ. He was tempted in every way like we are! If not, He couldn't be our substitute on the cross!

> *For we have not an high priest which cannot be touched with the feeling of our infirmities; but was in all points tempted like as we are, yet without sin. (Hebrews 4:15)*

Emotions *are* a gift from God, but if we take them out of their proper place and allow ourselves to be led by them, our emotions can take us in wrong directions. The enemy can easily manipulate our emotions by manipulating our outward circumstances. So if we are led by our feelings, we are basically at the mercy of the devil (and as we know, he has no mercy).

OUR FIRST LOVE

There is a very powerful force that God pours out on the face of the earth through His people. It is His unconditional love, energized and empowered by our feelings and emotions. In fact, Jesus talks about the first love to the Church in Ephesus in Revelation 2:4:

> *Nevertheless I have somewhat against thee, because thou hast left thy first love. (Revelation 2:4)*

By "love" He doesn't mean something mental or rational. He is talking about an emotional, passionate, on-fire love for Him. It is very much like the love we experienced for our spouse when we first met them, first married them or first started our relationship with them. That love was so powerful that the force of that love set agendas for us. It moved us out of our comfort zone and made us willing to do anything necessary to fulfill the passionate desire we had to be with our mate.

The word *love* refers to passion and to affection. When our feelings and emotions come under the Lordship of

Jesus and they flow through us in a way that glorifies God, we can embrace God more fully than we ever did before. We make Him a priority in our lives because of this passion. These pure emotions help us make right decisions because we are driven by passion and love. The force of love that God has placed inside of us now directs and guides us in the path of righteousness. This passion focuses our thoughts on Him throughout the day. We will even get up early to pray and read His Word.

But, the devil also uses a counterfeit force. He cannot counterfeit love so he comes up with another strong emotion to misdirect us. He will use the passion of anger, the force of anger. It too will grab hold of our emotions but it takes us away from God and leads us in the direction that satan wants to bring us. We end up in places we ought not to be in. It is a real force and a real passion. It is misguided and misdirected, but it is indeed there. He will do everything he can to bring us into this place of anger and rage.

COUNTERFEIT PASSION VS GODLY PASSION

Be ye angry, and sin not: let not the sun go down on your wrath, nor give place to the devil. And grieve not the holy Spirit of God, whereby ye are sealed unto the day of redemption. Let all bitterness, wrath, anger, clamor, and evil speaking be put away from you, with all malice. (Ephesians 4:26, 30, 31)

Too often our feelings and emotions are separated from God's influence because of the sin in our lives. That is why anger can rise up so easily in our hearts. We say we "see red" because anger clouds our mind, takes control of our passion and leads us to make wrong choices and go in wrong directions. When we experience passionate anger with all of its ugly feelings and emotions of retribution it is from the wrong spirit and source! We believe that anger is the emotion that is the counterfeit passion for love. It is stirred up and inflamed by demonic forces. The enemy knows this so he tries to bring the counterfeit in. He wants to separate us from God and draw us away to play in his ballpark. He has been pretty successful, just look around you.

"You took my _____ (you fill in the blank). You don't understand. That's *my* _____! What's the matter with you?" We get passionate over the silliest, stupidest things because the devil has stolen our passion for God and perverted it into anger. This opens up the door for a spirit of anger.

There is a difference between feeling the emotion of anger and having a spirit of anger demonize you. You may be asking yourself, "Is he implying that a Christian can be possessed?" It is true that, as a Christian, you can no longer be possessed by demons, but you can be demonized. That means that they affect you in many ways and have a great influence on your life. Many times we pray for Christians and they will drop to the floor in a fetal position, trembling, shaking or displaying some other manifestation of deliverance. When it's over, they feel embarrassed and may ask, "Oh my God I am saved, aren't I? Why is this happening to me?" Yes they are. This happened because demonic powers had their hooks inside their soul. The enemy found an inroad and, somewhere along the line, their feelings and emotions overtook them. If we live in a constant state of anger, demon spirits can come upon us, grab hold of us and spin our lives out of control. In the beginning we controlled the anger a little bit. We could hide it. We could just go into the closet and punch the wall. But when we are demonized, we can't help it anymore. Now, even in public we act out of control (like a demon).

On the other hand, when we sing to God in worship we can sense another kind of passion rising up, but this time it is from a holy source. His presence creates such a force inside of us that we yearn for more and more of Him. If we just bathe ourselves in His glory, the voice of the Holy Spirit will direct us to make good choices and decisions. God wants our emotions to draw us closer to Him, and to keep our priorities in order. The force of our love for Him makes us willing to go to church even when the wind is blowing, the rain is beating down or the sun is shining. We even linger after service at the altar to worship. We say, "I am not leaving until I touch the hem of His garment." Passion causes us to go way beyond ourselves.

Jesus says in Luke 4:18:

> *The Spirit of the Lord is upon me, because he hath anointed me to preach the gospel to the poor; he hath sent me to heal the broken-hearted, to preach deliverance to the captives, and recovering of sight to the blind, to set at liberty them that are bruised.*

The word for "heart" in Greek is *kardia* which directly refers to our feelings and emotions. Jesus came specifically to heal us and set us free from emotional bondage. He came to show us how to avoid the anger trap so we won't keep falling into the same problem over and over. Of course, outbursts of anger don't happen all the time, but they will rise up at the most inopportune times. They will take us off track and guide us away from God. God intends our feelings and emotions to be under the influence of the Holy Spirit so they will lead us closer to Him, not further away. But when they are controlled by our flesh, they lead us further away. We find ourselves ashamed, embarrassed and always having to say "I'm sorry."

BLINDED BY ANGER

I (Gaspar) know a story about a young man who had a terrible temper. He was very angry toward his wife. He had very deep hurts. **When we have hurt inside it creates anger.** For a number of years this couple battled and hurt each other until she finally surrendered to Christ and was set free from her anger issues. He was still very hurt and angry, but refused to turn his life over to the Lord and allow Him to heal his wounds.

One day when his wife went to church, his anger got the best of him. Of course, he didn't go to church with her. I am sure he was sitting all alone in his house, listening to the voice of the enemy; fueling his anger and rage. Passionate anger was now controlling him to do something that was outside the will of God. He drove his car to his wife's church and left a note on her car telling her that, by the time she got back home, he would have killed himself. With retaliation and rebellion in his heart to punish his wife, he went home, took a gun, went into the bedroom and shot himself in the head!

She came home and found him dead. However, from the evidence, it was obvious that he didn't die right away. After he had shot himself, he dropped the gun and ran into the bathroom. He had tried to stop the bleeding by stuffing toilet paper in the wound and to call an ambulance.

Old hurts allowed the anger, passion and wrath to take hold of his life and it spurred him to do this horrible thing. Yet, after he shot himself, I am sure that he heard a demonic voice saying, "Look what you did! What a fool!" He probably said, "Oh my God! I made a mistake. Let me try to help myself!" But it was too late.

Although this story is quite dramatic, it shows how the enemy operates in all of us if we let him control our passions. How many times have we done something, said something or went someplace in a fit of rage, full of anger and hatred toward someone, without thinking of the consequences?

> But he that hateth his brother is in darkness, and walketh in darkness, and knoweth not whither he goeth, because that darkness hath blinded his eyes. (I John 2:11)

The Holy Spirit is saying that hatred and anger cause us to walk in darkness and we don't even know where we are going! They blind us. Have you ever been so furious that you jumped in the car and started speeding down the road? When you think about it afterward, don't you feel kind of foolish for taking such a risk with your life and the lives of the people around you? Have you ever been so angry with someone that you said the meanest, cruelest thing you could think of to them and then after the feeling subsided, after the storm calmed down you just wanted to crawl in a hole because you felt so bad?

It's funny how the devil will pull back the veil after he gets you to do his bidding. This is not a new modus operandi! In the Garden, at the fall of man, the serpent was cunning and deceptive, playing with Adam and Eve's emotions. After they made the terrible choice to act on the will of their emotions, rather than God's will, they realized that they were naked and ashamed. Just like us. **After we let our emotions dictate our actions, satan accuses us and we feel naked and ashamed!**

These out of control emotions are a strong force, and the Lord has come to heal us from them. He wants us to harness them under His Lordship and use them the right way so we will be passionately in love with Jesus. So we will

141

love Him and be willing to go out of our way to tell someone else about Him. It has nothing to do with how comfortable we "feel" or don't "feel." "I just love you so much Lord. My body, mind and my soul will serve You by telling someone about Your love." We need the passion of the Lord to do that.

Let's go back again to the analogy of that wonderful, first love we had for our mate. When we first met that special someone and fell in love, we were so excited! That person just consumed our thoughts, night and day! What passion! We showed their picture to everyone; over and over again we read their love-letters. The people around us got so bored hearing how wonderful we think our beloved one is! That is how we should feel about Jesus, our wonderful Savior! He is the "Lover of our Soul!" He is the lifter of our head! He loves us with an everlasting, unconditional love. The Bible is a "picture" of who God is. The Bible is the passionate love-letter He has written to us! Let's read it over and over again. Share it with everyone! Face it; can any person on this earth love us like He does? He is the One who deserves our deepest passion!

OPEN DOORS -FREE ACCESS TO THE ENEMY!

The devil will twist and pervert our passion when he finds an open door. He is looking for the open door of "hurt." Our feelings of anger can be traced back to a time in our life when we experienced a hurt. The devil works through our areas of hurt. Let me give you an example. Do you have children? Have you played with a child? You roll on the floor having a good time when all of a sudden they poke you in the eye or do something else that suddenly causes pain. You are playing, they make a mistake, you are hurt and you grab them and yell, "What are you doing?"

They didn't know what they were doing. They accidentally poked you in the eye. They didn't mean it. But because you were hurt, the very next thing that was triggered was the passion of anger. You end up shaking inside when it is all over. You reacted the very instant it happened because it hurt.

Old hurts that were never healed give access to the devil. They are spawning places for this emotion of anger and will cause us to "see red." It doesn't happen all the time but when it does happen we just lose it! We say things we don't want to say and do things we don't want to do. Later, when the devil lifts the veil and starts taunting us for what he just did through us, it is too late, the damage has been done. (Like that young man who took his own life.) We can't take back the behavior and it winds up becoming multiplied over and over again. We feel so embarrassed that we avoid the people who saw us acting like an angry fool!

We need to close the open doors of old hurts.

The spirit of a man will sustain his infirmity; but a wounded spirit who can bear? (Proverbs 18:14)

Keep thy heart with all diligence; for out of it are the issues of life. (Proverbs 4:23)

You ask, "How can my spirit be wounded?" God gave you the authority to keep or guard your spirit just as He gave Adam the authority to protect the Garden of Eden in Genesis 2:15:

And the LORD God took the man, and put him into the Garden of Eden to dress it and to keep it. (Genesis 2:15)

One of the meanings of the word "keep" (*shamar* in Hebrew) is to guard from an outside invasion. Why did God tell him to "keep" it, to guard it? After all, they were in

Paradise, a place of perfection! What or who did Adam have to guard against? Satan was not manifested in the garden yet, so man was able to walk in the cool of the day with the Lord. There was close intimacy between man and his Creator. God met every one of man's needs in the garden. The trees were fully blossomed, the waters were filled with fishes and God gave Adam dominion over everything, even the creeping things on the earth. God was aware of the plans of satan, and He warned Adam. But, he didn't heed God's command to guard the garden. The enemy came in through the back door and the garden was destroyed.

God tells us to keep our spirit. We need Him to restore us and heal our wounds. It is up to us to make the commitment to 'keep' our spirit so the enemy cannot cause anger to rise up in us again. That is how we can avoid the trap of the devil. A wounded spirit provides fertile soil for the enemy to plant seeds of hatred and anger. Diligently guarding our spirit means that we do not bring all of the bad hurtful incidents back to our memory. We can't let our heart remain in a state of unforgiveness. Guarding with diligence means watching what we listen to, what we see, who we associate with. We need to take inventory of our life every day because if our spirit is wounded we will not have the strength necessary to resist during the times of attack and oppression from the enemy.

If our spirit is strong, when the wind and the rain come we will remain standing because we are on the solid rock of Jesus Christ. A healed spirit will get us through the toughest times of our life. But if our spirit is weak, when pressure comes we will fall apart because as a man is on the inside so shall he be on the outside. Visualize a plastic container. If an outside force tries to crush it, it needs to exert greater pressure on the outside of the container than the pressure that is inside the container. We are like that container. There are forces outside of us that want to crush us, but remember what it says in I John 4:4:

Ye are of God, little children, and have overcome them: because greater is he that is in you, than he that is in the world.

We have the Greater One living inside of us. God has shown us that our spirit will sustain our infirmities, but we cannot withstand the pressures that come against us if we have a wounded spirit (inner weakness). These wounds are deep because of sin. The major sin is unforgiveness that brings roots of bitterness. Now there is an open door for satan to plant his seeds of hatred and anger in us. What a set up! We end up being a problem to ourselves and everyone else around us.

Whoever has no rule over his own spirit is like a city broken down without walls. (Proverbs 25:28)

He who is slow to anger is better than the mighty, and he who rules his spirit than he who takes a city. (Proverbs 16:32)

We think these scriptures sum up what we are saying. Our defenses are weakened when we allow anger to rule us. When we are out of control the enemy has free access to our life. On the other hand, when we are slow to anger we are strong and can resist the enemy.

WORSHIP PRODUCES GODLY PASSION

Praise brings us into the outer court but worship brings us into the Holy of Holies where we can stand in the presence of the Lord, face to face. When you are alone, do you ever put on a worship tape or CD? This allows the presence of God to come forth inside you and rivers of living water to flow through you and around you. As Moses struck the

145

rock and the water came out, God wants to strike your spirit and release His love again.

When you begin to recognize that truth, you will sense and perceive it in your heart. It will make a big difference in your attitude and your countenance. It will make a difference in your life. People won't even recognize you. Remember when you first got saved? People said that you looked different. There was a glow on your face. Did anyone say that to you? They noticed something; what was it? The life that was present in your spirit was coming out. You still dressed the same, you still combed your hair the same, put on your makeup the same and walked the same. What were they seeing? They were seeing the life of Christ flowing out of your spirit. Did you ever notice someone who, when they first got saved they looked bright and beautiful, but then the next time you met them you saw a cloud of darkness over them? Their face and countenance changed. Before long they were backslidden because the light in their spirit went out and the life flow from the Spirit of God through their spirit had stopped. These things are observable in the natural world. Do you think it is worth taking the time to worship Him? My answer is, "Yes!" He wants to stir up a passion in our heart. He wants to transform the passion of anger into the passion of love so it will direct our priorities and position us to allow the supernatural power of God to flow through us.

DROP THE FIG LEAVES

When we get a touch from the Father's hand, the walls of separation come down and we become vulnerable and transparent before God. Some of us are trying to hide ourselves and don't want anyone to really know us because we want people to just see our good side. We even do that with

STOP HURTING START HEALING

God because we feel that if He sees our bad side He will reject us. We are like Adam and Eve when they put on their fig leaves in the Garden of Eden and hid from God. We try to cover ourselves and hide from Him and from people. We don't get close to anyone because we are afraid that they will witness our outbursts of anger. We can stay in control in a big crowd, but we allow no one to get close to us. We imagine in our hearts, "If you get to know me you won't like me and I am afraid of that." We do the same thing with God. We may not consciously realize it but subconsciously that is what happens, and it limits how far we will go in our worship. We will press in to a point, but when we start to get emotional, we panic and say, "No, I can't have any tears come down my eyes. I have to make sure my tie is straight/my makeup is fine. I have to be in control and look good."

When we hide behind the fig leaf, we are afraid to drop it even for an instant. We hinder God from coming inside of us to heal the deep wounded areas. His perfect love will cast out our fear. The best way to allow Him to heal our hurt is by worshiping Him with abandon. Cast your cares to the wind and don't be concerned about how long it takes or how many people see you. People are sometimes critical and say it is getting too wild in the church. They are not worshiping the Lord because if they were, their eyes would be on Him and not people. Don't worry about other people, don't get distracted, just set your affection on Him! Our passion level needs to rise up until we won't care about anyone else's opinion. If we want this healing it will come through worshiping God. There is no shortcut! He is the Great Physician and He can go where no knife can go. If we don't let Him heal our hearts we will find ourselves being led astray.

Anger is the number one force that satan works through, but God's force works through divine forgiveness and unconditional love. The devil uses anger, hatred and bitterness. He wants to control us and make a mess of our life. When we walk in anger we become a servant of the devil rather than of God. When we walk in God's love, we are God's servant. We can't have it both ways. I Peter 5:8 says:

> Be sober, be vigilant; because your adversary the devil, as a roaring lion, walketh about, seeking whom he may devour.

Satan stirs up the passion that rightfully belongs to God. If he can get a grip on us, his spirit influences us, and our lives will be out of order.

> He who is quick-tempered acts foolishly. (Proverbs 14:17)

Our quick temper will make us act in an ungodly manner. If our passion and emotions are under the influence of Christ's love and His Lordship, we glorify Him.

We need to love the Lord with all our heart, soul, mind and strength. Loving Him with everything we have pleases Him. When that happens, the supernatural will come through us. When love flows through us, healing takes place because it comes from inside. Rivers of living waters come out of our innermost being. They are rivers of God's love. When we give out His love, our mind, our thoughts, our feelings, our issues and our hurts get healed. He says we should be sober, vigilant and alert to what is going on around us. Be aware of the set-ups. The main reason we still have hurt can often be traced to unforgiveness that turns into roots of bitterness. We can never get healed from our hurts until we release those who hurt us through the act of forgiveness. So much time may have elapsed from the initial hurt, that all we have left is pain. We need to realize that it is a fruit with deep roots. It is just as simple as that. We may not recognize it but it is there. It is proof positive that if we see fruit, it has to be connected to a root. As long as hurts are coming forth as anger, we know that there is still unforgiveness in us. It needs to be released. Let's find out the truth of what happened, by asking the Holy Spirit. He guides us into all truth.

RIGHTEOUS ANGER

Be ye angry, and sin not: let not the sun go down upon your wrath. (Ephesians 4:26)

"Righteous anger" seems like a contradiction but it isn't. There is a right time to express an extreme passion and feel a hatred for the things that God hates and actually despise what He despises. Righteous anger comes from a completely different source. It comes out of His love, His source. It is out of concern, compassion and loyalty to who God is. It is coming out of His holiness. It is different from this other destructive force of anger. Righteous anger is constructive. It will bring life and will help others. It helps us not to compromise. You would be surprised at how many Christians try to do a balancing act. They are in the middle of the road and don't have a passion for God at all. When they choose to take the easy way, making it simple and full of compromise they figure, "no big deal." But when we begin to hate what God hates we begin to see those very things in our own lives first. We bring correction to ourselves and get the beam out of our own eye. Then we can be an example to those who need to receive correction from God. That is our call. We are to witness, testify and bring forth the truth, but the best way is through our own lifestyles.

We cannot correct somebody if we still live the same way they do. We will have to keep our mouth shut. But when the passion of God is flowing through our lives, we have a righteous anger and we will want to separate from those things. Then, by our lifestyle we can bring conviction and correction to someone else. This is righteous anger versus an evil unrighteous anger... there is a big difference. God's Spirit stirs up a righteous anger, and the other is stirred up by an evil spirit.

BLOODLINES: ANOTHER OPEN DOOR FOR ANGER

Keeping mercy for thousands, forgiving iniquity and transgression and sin, and that will by no means clear the guilty; visiting the iniquity of the fathers upon the children, and upon the children's children, unto the third and to the fourth generation. (Exodus 34:7)

God was revealing some things to Moses. He was revealing that iniquities of past generations are passed down through the bloodlines. This is another issue we need to examine as we strive to get free from anger and its destructive force in our life.

Our fathers have sinned, [and are] not; and we have borne their iniquities. (Lamentations 5:7)

What is iniquity? It is the power of the force behind sin. It is the defectiveness of character that produces the sin. Although we may not have committed that sin, we have the power and force to do it. There are some things that pass down to us from our father, grandfather etc. that are not good. They have become part of our personality, are embedded in us and we struggle with these "iniquity drives." Eventually, at the right time, with the right trap, the right scenario and the right force, anger surfaces and we do something that causes the iniquity to become a sin in our lives. Just like that plastic container we talked about, when the pressure comes, we are faced with a conflict. This iniquity can take hold of us and the anger can bring us in the wrong direction.

The wages of sin is death. Most of what is happening in our lives can be identified and tracked in the past. We need to look at this and see if there are any open doors through our bloodlines. Was there any anger or violence in my family? Were there suicidal thoughts in our family, or verbal abuse? Am I just repeating what has been done before in past generations? Great deliverance is accomplished by applying the blood of Jesus Christ to break the bloodlines of our natural fathers and grandfathers etc., going back to the fourth generation. Why only the fourth generation? Because the law of sowing and reaping increases at the rate of thirty, sixty and a hundred fold. By the time it gets to the fourth generation, if not dealt with, the effects of the bloodline will consume that generation. Some family lines have been wiped out from drugs, alcohol, gambling, etc. The iniquity began many years ago and it is now in the fourth generation. Fortunately, the law of sowing and reaping also works conversely to bring positive results. Families that have been 'true' Christians, obeying Godly principles for three or four generations, are experiencing the abundant life today.

They are more advanced in the things of God because their heritage has been multiplied in a positive way. An example of a Godly heritage is the famous preacher Jonathan Edwards, (third generation of a family of Pastors) who sparked a tremendous spiritual revival in the 1700's. Bloodlines are a key. Look back at your family heritage and see if it is contributing to your anger problem.

TRANSFERENCE OF SPIRITS

We must acknowledge that demonic powers walk the face of this earth. They try to attach themselves to us. In his letter to the church at Ephesus, the Apostle Paul wrote about the spiritual forces they were battling.

> *Finally, my brethren, be strong in the Lord, and in the power of his might. Put on the whole armour of God, that ye may be able to stand against the wiles of the devil. For we wrestle not against flesh and blood, but against principalities, against powers, against the rulers of the darkness of this world, against spiritual wickedness in high places. (Ephesians 6:10-12)*

Demonic spirits will literally jump on you, will transfer their nature to you and begin to work in your life through your feelings and emotions. Associate with an angry person for a period of time and eventually you are going to be just as angry as they are.

Years ago, I (Michele) was counseling a woman who had tremendous anger. Her husband abandoned her, abused her and constantly drank. He was a drug addict and alcoholic. After living like that for a number of years, she was angry and bitter. In fact, a force of anger raged inside of her. I counseled her a couple of times in a row. I really wanted to help, so I spent a lot of time with her. One day when my husband came home, I had just finished counseling this woman and all of a sudden I started treating him like a villain. I started talking to him in a very angry tone. He thought, "What did I do?"

The Lord showed him that there was a transference of spirits. I had just finished counseling with this woman and the same angry demon spirit that was attacking her, causing her to be so vicious toward her husband, was now influencing me. It is a real force, a real power. We prayed, broke it and learned that we needed to pray a cleansing prayer whenever we were in situations involving demonic powers, which is every day.

When we (not just Pastors) go home, we need to ask, "Why do I have this particular thought? Why do I have this particular desire? It doesn't seem to be me. Where did it come from?" It is likely that the people we were hanging around had that same spirit. Now we are influenced also because we were with them The spirit transferred to us either through their words or through their touch. When dating, people need to be careful about touching or lighting each other's fire.

When lives become enmeshed, unclean spirits can be transferred and will control and manipulate us. The good news is that it is also true in the reverse. We may drag ourselves into church with a bad attitude, not wanting to be there, but by the time we leave we are praising the Lord. Hallelujah! We are dancing around and happy. What happened? There was a good transference of spirits. We come to church feeling down and out and cold-hearted and leave happy, hopeful and on-fire.

Make no friendship with an angry man; and with a furious man thou shalt not go: Lest thou learn his ways, and get a snare to thy soul. (Proverbs 22:24, 25)

First Corinthians15:33 says:

Be not deceived: evil communications corrupt good manners.

Make no friends with an angry man and don't hang around with a furious man. Why? So we won't learn his ways and get caught up in them. Evil communication or companionship will wind up corrupting us. A little leaven spoils the whole lump. Put one good apple in a bunch of bad apples and what happens? The good apple turns bad. Take one bad apple and put it in a bunch of good apples and what happens? All the good apples turn bad. The force of evil on the face of the earth is strong.

A violent man enticeth his neighbour, and leadeth him into the way that is not good. (Proverbs 16:29)

Anger can very easily be transferred. If we continue on in that realm, it will find open doors in our lives and cause this onslaught of demonic powers to control us.

Be not hasty in thy spirit to be angry: for anger resteth in the bosom of fools. (Ecclesiastes 7:9)

Once the force of the passion of anger is released, it will make us do things that we don't even want to do. Even put a gun to our head, like that husband I spoke about!

Let me tell you what my life was like as a young man before I (Gaspar) came to Christ. Now remember, I wasn't saved! I was out with a bunch of guys and we thought we had a right to rip off things because we were angry. Don't ask me why we were angry; there was no logical reason except that we were like puppets on a string being used by demonic forces to bring destruction. We were just angry macho guys, walking around putting holes in things, breaking in and stealing stuff. We stole the tires off a big truck one night, because we knew we could sell them for three or four hundred dollars each. We got under the rig, jacked it up and got ready to take the tire off when, all of a sudden, the axle flipped off the jack and it came down and just missed my head.

I could have instantly been crushed to death! The anger was driving me to do something evil. The enemy was using my friends' influence to lead me down his path. Satan wanted to kill me. He didn't care what I did; he just wanted to kill me. Do you understand that he wants to kill you too and take you to hell? He wants us to miss our destiny;

STOP HURTING START HEALING

that is what it is all about. It's all about death, destruction and misery.

> *The thief cometh not, but for to steal, and to kill, and to destroy.* (John 10:10a)

ANGER TROUBLES US AND DEFILES MANY

Hebrews 12:14, 15 says:

> *Follow peace with all men, and holiness, without which no man shall see the Lord: follow peace with all men. Looking diligently lest any man fail of the grace of God; lest any root of bitterness springing up trouble you, and thereby many be defiled.*

In other words walk the journey of divine forgiveness, looking for places of agreement, bringing your hurt or your fault to your brother so you can win them, so you can enter into God's power plant, "where two or three are gathered together." The Body of Christ, His church, wasn't even birthed until they were all together in unity in the Upper Room!

> *And when the day of Pentecost was fully come, they were all with one accord in one place. (Acts 2:1)*

Always look for peace, always look to release divine forgiveness, don't build walls or tear down relationships. Look for things to agree on. Why?

> *Looking diligently lest any man fail of the grace of God....* (Hebrews 12:15)

What is the grace of God? Unconditional love. When we fail to forgive somebody it's because we are ignorant of what Jesus Christ has done for us. God looks at us through the eyes of Jesus Christ. That is how we are supposed to look at everybody who has hurt us. If we don't, we have failed at the grace of God. We have failed to realize all that He has done for us. Then what happens? He says:

Lest any root of bitterness springing up trouble you... many be defiled. (Hebrews 12:15)

The first thing bitterness will do is trouble us. Trouble can manifest in many ways: sickness and disease, our personality, our relationships, etcetera. We can also become withdrawn and angry.

It not only troubles you, but you become a "troublemaker" and others are affected. They say as they scatter, "Here he comes, watch out!" Have you noticed that when you come around everybody scatters? That is because you have now become so defiled by bitterness, jealousy, envy, a mocking spirit, and anger; that it can't be contained anymore. These things damage us and cause sickness and disease in our bodies. Our thoughts become distorted and the flow of Christ's love through us is hindered. We can't even see the good that is inside of us, or the good things that God has provided for us. This attitude consumes our personality and now wherever we go and open our mouth we end up creating problems. Everything around us becomes a problem because we are so irritable. This proves that our heart is not pure because our attitude is just the opposite of what is described in Titus 1:15a:

Unto the pure all things are pure.

The problem is that when "me" is the problem, "me" doesn't necessarily know it or want to admit it. All this makes us miserable from the time we wake up to the time we go to sleep, but we don't even know why!

A friend visited his grandfather in England and related this story. His grandfather's fingers were filled with arthritis and it caused him constant pain. The very first thing he spoke to his grandson about was how angry he was at his own sister. He was just wracked with pain in his arms and legs and he said, "She got the house!"

The incident he was talking about happened forty years ago. When his mother died she left the house to his sister and gave him nothing. He never got over it and he was so bitter. "I don't know if she's dead or not but I know she got the house!" If you ask him how he is doing, all he can do is talk about his sister. And here he was with his fingers like hooks. Many people suffer from arthritis, which is frequently caused by bitterness. Of course, it's not the only cause but it is one of the major reasons people have this disease.

We were praying for a woman a while ago and the Lord gave us a "word of knowledge". We were praying for her to be healed from stomach cancer and arthritis in her hands. The Lord told us to ask her if she had forgiven her husband. We were praying for the healing of her body, but the Holy Spirit wanted us to pray for her to forgive. She said, "How do you know I am still angry at my husband and I haven't ever forgiven him?" She agreed to forgive him at that moment, without hesitation. As we prayed, her hands began to open, just by forgiving. She came back three weeks later and told us that she was healed of the cancer in her stomach. It is a true story. She was healed of the stomach cancer because it was rooted in bitterness. We can't say that every disease is rooted in bitterness, but over the years we have observed a correlation and the medical community is beginning to support that view as well.

HOW SOUL TIES AFFECT US

Looking diligently lest any man fail of the grace of God; lest any root of bitterness springing up trouble you, and thereby many be defiled. (Hebrews 12:15)

This scripture says that many will be defiled by us if we have a root of bitterness. That's very serious. We know that like spirits attract, or as the world says, "Birds of a feather flock together." In church there are certain people who attract others to themselves because they al share 'roots of bitterness.' Cliques form. You can identify them by their attitude and the spirits that operate in them. These 'people connections' are called soul ties. Because we are affected by the people we associate with, the Lord gave us these instructions in II Corinthians 6:17:

> Wherefore come out from among them, and be ye separate, saith the Lord, and touch not the unclean thing; and I will receive you.

Familiar spirits tie our soul together with others and we become dependent and co-dependent on a particular person or group for advice. In the church we have "spiritual mothers and fathers." In many instances it's just an excuse for witchcraft, manipulation and control. We hear people say, "I'm going to my spiritual mother to see what she says." I say, "Go to the Bible!" so they don't hear things like, "I don't think you should marry him because..." It is control and manipulation.

We are not saying that we shouldn't give godly advice to one another. But, along with our opinions, we need to first encourage people to hear from the Holy Spirit directly rather than from us, or from any man. They will answer, "I love that pastor, and I won't do anything unless I hear it from the pastor."

I am a pastor and I say, "Don't do that!" You need to hear from God. Even when we preach from the pulpit, you need to go back and check it with the Holy Spirit. That is what God wants. We have too many soul ties and they influence our views. So-and-so is angry with her husband, and now she is giving you advice on how to treat your husband. God forbid! What she can't accomplish in her own marriage, she's going to accomplish in yours? Before you know it, there is a manifestation of anger coming forth in you. These are demonic influences.

We even find certain effects from geographical places. There are specific strongholds in different geographical areas. We can travel to one place where it is wonderfully built up, beautifully kept, all the properties are nice, and everything is fine. Then we go to another neighborhood and observe that everything is run down and broken. This happens because demons have an influence over the people of a region.

ANGRY PEOPLE: FRIENDS OF THE ENEMY

And it came to pass as they came, when David was returned from the slaughter of the Philistine, that the women came out of all cities of Israel, singing and dancing, to meet king Saul, with tabrets, with joy, and with instruments of musick. And the women answered one another as they played, and said, Saul hath slain his thousands, and David his ten thousands. And Saul was very wroth, and the saying displeased him; and he said, They have ascribed unto David ten thousands, and to me they have ascribed but thousands: and what can he have more but the kingdom? And Saul eyed David from that day and forward. (I Samuel 18:6-9)

Saul got jealous. All of a sudden he wasn't 'numero uno' anymore, and now they were building up David instead of him. That jealousy stirred up Saul's passions and made him very, very angry. He was already angry with Samuel because he would not forgive a sin he committed previously. Actually the bottom line was that he was really angry with God.

God wanted him to do things one way and he thought that God didn't know what was best, so he did it his own

159

way. He thought his way would be accepted and he made excuses to Samuel about his actions, but God rejected his way. I believe he had anger against God in his heart because God did not accept his repentance. We know that God looks at what is in the heart of man. Saul had anger, jealousy and hatred in his heart just like Cain, who killed his own brother. Saul was angry with God, with Samuel and then we see that he was angry with David. He was just an angry man.

> *And it came to pass on the morrow, that the evil spirit from God came upon Saul, and he prophesied in the midst of the house: and David played with his hand, as at other times: and there was a javelin in Saul's hand. (I Samuel 18:10)*

We see that this anger brought forth an evil spirit. We cannot allow our unbridled anger to be so much a part of us that we open a door to an evil spirit. We cannot remain in that dangerous condition.

> *Cease from anger, and forsake wrath; do not fret, it only causes harm. (Psalm 37:8)*

When we feed the passion of anger, it grows. Worldly therapists will say, "You just need to be free to express yourself. Get rid of the inhibitions in your life. Come to my office. I have a punching bag that you can put your husband's face on, punch him out and get rid of the anger!"

You aren't getting rid of anger! You are simply enhancing and confirming it. What you feed grows! The therapists say you can punch him in their office and then love him when you get home, but I don't agree! When you go home, you forget that you are not in the therapist's office and you punch him there too! Then you say, "Oh, I thought I was at the office! Sorry, honey, I got confused. I didn't mean that!" Colossians 2:8 warns us about following man's philosophy:

Beware lest any man spoil you through philosophy and vain deceit, after the tradition of men, after the rudiments of the world, and not after Christ.

We need to get to the roots. As long as there is legal ground (roots) the enemy will fight you. You can rebuke him, but he will say, "I have legal ground." He is an attorney; he knows his rights.

ANGER BLINDS US

He who is slow to wrath has great understanding, but he who is impulsive exalts folly. (Proverbs 14:29)

Anger will cloud our view of God. Look at the story of Saul of Tarsus. He was breathing out fire as he persecuted the early Christians, (they were Jews). He was a very high-ranking and politically connected Pharisee. Along comes "The Way," making the religious Jews all upset. Everything Saul ever did was now being challenged and it made him angry. Sometimes the truth can really get us angry. (We go in one direction for so long that we think we are living the right way, but it is really just folly.) God suddenly shows us the right thing and we get angry because our foundation was shaken, and we do not want to let go of it. We fear that if we let go of the foundation, we will let go of our identity. God wants to do away with that identity and give us a new identity in Christ. It is the truth that makes us free!

In Philippians, Paul says that since he was saved and the veils are off of his eyes, he counts all the things he knew before as dung. Before he was saved, he was angry with the Christians. So he persecuted and killed them. He had veils on his eyes. He couldn't see, and his view of life was clouded. His idea of what should be done for God and how to do it was clouded. Anger clouds our thinking and confuses us.

161

We think we are rational, but we are irrational. We are drawing conclusions based on faulty perceptions just like the young man that shot himself in the head. He had no hope of his marriage being healed. All he saw was "It's over. I'll get her. I'll kill myself!"

> *Blessed are they that have a pure heart for they shall see God.* (Matthew 5:8)

We cannot see, experience, or know God unless our heart is pure. If our vision is not pure, it will be distorted and affect everything we do.

MAKE THE RIGHT CHOICE!

Some of us today have a clouded view; we do not see the destiny God has given us. We are hopeless and in despair. Everyday it gets worse because we are angry, even with God. We say "God, why didn't you do it my way? How come? I'm doing the best I can. I'm trying to make this work. Why aren't you doing it my way?" He is God and we are not. It is that plain and simple. He is the Alpha and the Omega; He is the beginning and the end. He knows how it turns out before we even get there. We are trying to force God to do what we want Him to do instead of what He has already done.

> *And hope maketh not ashamed; because the love of God is shed abroad in our hearts by the Holy Ghost which is given unto us.* (Romans 5:5)

Our only hope of finding freedom from anger is through the release of God's love in our hearts. The Holy Spirit is the source of this passion, this love, and this fire. We need to allow Him to dwell deep within us. A soulish Christian is more open to the spirit of anger and its influence. Let us decide to discipline and crucify our flesh and see the force of God's love come forth in our life. Join me in resolving to turn the passion of anger into the passion and zeal of the Lord! Let us commit to continue in this love walk. Let us return to our FIRST LOVE, our FIRST PASSION!

PRAY THIS PRAYER:

Lord, baptize me with not only the Holy Spirit, but also with Fire as You say in Your Word. Now that I am not controlled by the passion of anger, I desire to be controlled by the passion of my first love for Jesus. My faith is in you, Lord Jesus, and I resist the temptation to be angry again. I am contagious with the baptism of fire, and the love for Jesus, my Lord and Savior, affects everybody with whom I come in contact. Even the passion of anger is no match for the fire of God's love in my life. Lord, help me to stay both in the fire and on fire as I worship you daily. Amen.

STUDY QUESTIONS

1. Would you describe your emotions as under the control of the flesh or the Spirit? If you answered "the flesh", write down some steps you can take to get them under the control of the Spirit of God.

2. Meditate on Proverbs 16:32. Write it out 3 times and commit it to memory.

3. After reading this chapter, are there any relationships you feel the Holy Spirit prompting you to end because of their negative influence on you? Which ones?

CHAPTER ELEVEN
PLUNDER THE ENEMY

At this point we have taken apart this issue of forgiveness and examined it from every angle. I pray that by now we truly understand what a crucial issue we are dealing with. So I say, let's roll up our "spiritual sleeves," get to work and see how to apply what we have learned! Let's dig for some "Holy Spirit" strategies that will set us free from the bondage of unforgiveness! Let's walk forward and possess the land! Jesus is asking, "Wilt thou be made whole?" Let's answer and say, "Yes, Jesus, I want to be made whole. Show me!"

COME OUT FROM AMONG THEM

Separate from hurtful relationships! This statement doesn't mean we shouldn't walk in love. The reality is, not everybody is going in the same direction that God is taking us. Remember that Abraham had to separate from Lot (Gen. 13:9). He couldn't see the promises of God until he separated from him. We have to separate from certain people because they are holding us back. Certain friends and relationships actually keep us from overcoming our problems because their lifestyle links us to our past and they sabotage our walk with God. If we separate from them, God will reveal the next step to us. We need to let Him prune some branches from our life so we can bear more fruit, fruit that remains. We need to break old soul ties with people we are codependent with and who keep us steeped in a negative atmosphere. Break those soul ties. They may be very loving, nice and caring (human love/human care), but the relationship is not producing God's life or bringing us into the vision that He has for us. Separate yourself from them so God can take you where He wants to.

Let me clarify this so I won't be misunderstood. When I say that we need to separate from people who are hindering our walk with God, I am not referring to a spouse. Some people in unhappy marriages believe that they can get divorced because their partner is not walking at the same level in God as they are. Guess what? God takes the marriage covenant very seriously and He expects us to forgive each other, love unconditionally and live in peace together. Why do you think God refers to Himself as the God of Abraham, Isaac and Jacob? It is because He cares about the generations and our spiritual heritage. Our family is our first ministry. God's Word says that the husband is supposed to lay down his life for his wife, like Jesus did for the church. And the wife is supposed to submit to her husband as unto the Lord. It is very simple! (It is a different scenario though if our spouse is forcing us to do something against God's Word.) I just don't want someone to say to me, "Pastor, thanks for the advice in your book about leaving my husband. He used to get so mad when I went to church three times a week and he was really hindering my walk with Jesus!" You know what I mean, right?

RECEIVE PRAYER

Is any sick among you? Let him call for the elders of the church; and let them pray over him, anointing him with oil in the name of the Lord: And the prayer of faith shall save the sick, and the Lord shall raise him up; and if he have committed sins, they shall be forgiven him. Confess your faults one to another, and pray one for another, that ye may be healed. The effectual fervent prayer of a righteous man availeth much. (James 5:13-15)

We need each other because there are certain things we can't resolve by ourselves. The anointing God placed in me will bless you, and the anointing He placed in you will bless me. That is why God releases a corporate blessing when we get into unity. That is why the enemy works so hard to keep Christians separated. He knows that when our hearts are unified, there is a great power flow that blesses all of us.

Prayer is a tool that God utilizes to bring deliverance in your life. Don't just call anybody to pray for you. Call people who have been tried and tested. Call for the elders to pray over you. "And the prayer of faith shall save the sick, and the Lord shall raise him up; and if he have committed sins, they shall be forgiven him. Confess [your] faults one to another, and pray one for another, that ye may be healed." We can see that there is a connection between sin and sickness. Open your hearts to prayer counseling that will identify the methods satan has used against you over the years. This type of prayer will cut the cords, break the bondage and will set you free. Receive prayer. Don't just try to go it alone. We need each other.

BECOME A WORSHIPPER

What does worship do? For one thing, it keeps us humble before God. There is a difference between worship and praise. There's nothing wrong with praise, but it's easy to praise through your soul (your mind, will and emotions). Your soul needs to praise God, but worship comes from your spirit because it doesn't necessarily start with your feelings. It comes out of purity of love, mercy and compassion. Praise is exciting. It's good to praise because God inhabits the praises of His people but He dwells with the worshippers. Worship is important to help us keep our life in God's flow. Worship produces holiness. Praise gets us into the outer courts but worship gets us into the Holy of Holies. There is a difference.

People come to our church and say they want more praise. That is good, but eventually we want to stay in the Holy of Holies. Throne Room Worship is where we want to stay. We want to be in His presence. To really worship there must be a brokenness of our flesh. We need to lift our hands, whether we feel like it or not. Bow down, lay prostrate before God. It doesn't matter what our flesh says. Our spirit says, "I Love You Lord. I want to worship You." When we are broken, we walk in divine forgiveness more readily because we learn how to live by our spirit and not our flesh. God wants us to walk the journey in order to accomplish this process. Unless the Lord builds a house, they that labor to build it, labor in vain.

SEVEN STEPS TO COMPLETE FORGIVENESS

After years of helping people deal with the issue of forgiveness in their lives, we have compiled a list of seven steps to help achieve the complete freedom that comes from releasing divine forgiveness. These steps sum up many of the points we have made in this book and will tie things together for you. I pray they will help you as they have helped others. These seven steps to complete forgiveness are not complete until all seven are followed. To walk in forgiveness, we have to take an inventory to see if we have followed through and fulfilled these seven steps:

STEP 1: TRUST THAT GOD WILL JUDGE RIGHTEOUSLY.

We can trust that God will not do the wrong thing. He will make sure that the person who hurt us receives retribution. But the retribution will be done in God's way, through love and mercy. God knows what it's going to take to turn that person around. We are not fighting against flesh and blood. That person is not our enemy. It is the demon spirit that has worked through them. Our forgiveness releases God's power to do battle against the forces of darkness that holds them captive. Sometimes we do more damage by *withholding* forgiveness from our loved ones than was done by the offense itself. It keeps them bound up in that sin.

> And when he had said this, he breathed on them, and saith unto them, Receive ye the Holy Ghost: Whosoever sins ye remit, they are remitted unto them; and whose soever sins ye retain, they are retained. (John 20:22, 23)

This passage shows the power that God gave us in forgiveness. The power of forgiving. When we forgive somebody, we literally wash away the sin that has been over their life that controlled them and opened the door for satan to keep them bound. **If we refuse to forgive, we are refusing to be Christ's ambassador.** We hurt our own cause—our own life—because the very person we want to be set free from is going to continue to stay bound and the devil will use them to continue to torment us. We have the power to forgive as Christ's ambassador. When we do, in the spirit realm legions of angels are released to come against the demonic powers and forces of darkness that have bound the person to that sin. And when they finally come to repent, they will receive the blessing of that freedom and be washed and healed by the blood of Jesus. Praise the Lord!

STEP 2: IT TAKES FAITH TO FORGIVE, NOT FEELINGS

If you are waiting for an ooey-gooey feeling to come over you before you say, "I forgive you", forget it. It's not going to happen. And if it does happen like that, it's only human forgiveness. We are talking about forgiveness in obedience and submission to God's Word.

We saw in a previous chapter that when Jesus told the disciples they should forgive over and over, they said, "Increase our faith". It is not about feelings; it is about faith. We are going to have to trust God. Faith is acting on God's Word. Faith is confessing God's Word. When we say "I forgive", with a true understanding of what Jesus Christ considers to be forgiveness, at that point in time, we are releasing faith. And faith moves mountains. We have to count the cost and then accept the cost, whether the person changes or not.

STEP 3: DENY YOURSELF

> *Then said Jesus unto his disciples, If any man will come after me, let him deny himself, and take up his cross, and follow me. (Matthew 16:24)*

If we are going to follow Christ and walk in forgiveness, we must deny ourselves, carry our cross so when the flesh rises up to do its own thing, we nail it on the cross and crucify it. Then we pick up our cross and go. Every time our feelings say *I am not going to forgive* lay them on the cross and crucify that flesh. Jesus did it all and forgave us even

170

before we received Him. You have given up the right to be right.

STEP 4: STOP ALL GOSSIP AND SOWING SEEDS OF DISCORD

A man's belly shall be satisfied with the fruit of his mouth; and with the increase of his lips shall he be filled. Death and life are in the power of the tongue: and they that love it shall eat the fruit thereof. (Proverbs 18:20, 21)

I think that many of us are eating some terribly bitter-tasting fruit. We need to start speaking words of life concerning our own situations, our lives and other people in our lives. If we do not have anything good to say, we should just shut up. Put your hand over your mouth, because once a word comes out of your mouth, it produces fruit. We need people around us who encourage us to speak God's Word. We need to surround ourselves with people who refuse to gossip and talk badly about other people.

When I say that we need to refuse to gossip, I mean that we are not going to bring up to another person what someone else has done to us. We have not really forgiven if we still talk about what the person did yet at the same time trying to look like such a great, holy-roller Christian. If we go around saying, "Yes, I took my husband back, I have forgiven him even though he hurt me again and even though he did all these things..." we have not extended divine forgiveness. Hurt people...hurt other people. When we are hurt, we try to knock someone else down to make ourselves feel better. That is just the way it is. That is human nature. Be careful of what comes out of your mouth because what you sow is what you reap. Many of us are planting a crop that will bring a negative harvest in the future. These spiritual laws work every time and in every situation whether we like it or not. We have to be very careful of the power of our words. So refuse to gossip!

STEP 5: AVOID GUILT TRIPS

Do not bring past offenses up to the person you forgave. Do not say things like "Look how I gave you your bedroom back." or "I just want to remind you that you did all these things…" Do not place a guilt trip on them. This is wrong. It is human forgiveness and it is not going to help anybody. Refuse to put the person on a guilt trip. Does God keep reminding us of all the sins we have committed against Him?

> There's no condemnation for those who walk in the spirit and not in the flesh. (Romans 8:1)

This is true for the person who forgives and the person who needed the forgiveness. So if you are walking in the flesh, you are going to bring condemnation to that person and place guilt on them.

STEP 6: GUARD YOUR MIND

Guarding our mind means not bringing up past memories and dwelling on them.

> Finally, brethren, whatsoever things are true, whatsoever things are honest, whatsoever things are just, whatsoever things are pure, whatsoever things are lovely, whatsoever things are of good report; if there be any virtue, and if there be any praise, think on these things. (Philippians 4:8)

The devil will bring up old offenses all the time and try to stir up our hearts. We have to be strong enough to rebuke the enemy because he still wants to develop strongholds in our thoughts so he can work through our minds. Our minds are the battleground of the devil. That is where the war is fought. It is either won or lost in the mind. When it comes to forgiveness, the battle is won or lost in the mind. We have to take a strong stand and say, "I refuse to allow this to come to my mind anymore." Because if it does, we are going to judge that person by his past and lose that forgiveness.

Can we lose forgiveness and cancel it out? Yes. We can divinely forgive and then take it back immediately and then we will have to 're-forgive'. Some of us have forgiven under the inspiration of the Holy Spirit, only to be attacked by the enemy, take the forgiveness back and gossip about it. So guard your mind and rebuke the enemy. Set your affections on things above. If you have been raised with Christ, then put your mind on Christ. Align your thoughts with His thoughts.

STEP 7: LOVE YOUR ENEMIES

We know we have really completed the forgiveness process—when we have reached the seventh step. Now we are totally restored with God and with that person.

> But I say unto you, Love your enemies, bless them that curse you, do good to them that hate you, and pray for them which despitefully use you, and persecute you. (Matthew 5:44)

Notice this verse does not say to love the people who treat us well or bless those who bless us. It does not say do good to those who do nice things for us or pray for those who pray for us. It says the total opposite. It says to love our enemies. You see, it takes nothing to love the person who is lovely, but it takes the supernatural to love our enemy. It takes nothing to do good for someone who is good to us. The highest form of human love is phileo. It is

173

where we get the word *philadelphia* (brotherly love). This kind of love says, "If you are nice to me, I will be nice to you. If you are kind to me, I will be kind to you. If you stop being nice to me, I will still be nice to you. If you stop being nice to me for a few days, it is over!"

Unconditional love (agape) says, "If you are nice to me, I will be nice to you. If you stop being nice to me, I will still be nice to you. If you hate me, I am still going to be nice to you. If you kick me in the shin, I will still be nice to you. If you spit in my face, I will still be nice to you." That is unconditional love. God is telling us to love our enemies unconditionally. We can not do this in the natural realm, only in the spiritual. Bless those who curse you.

When we have really forgiven someone, we are going to be able to pray for them. Unconditional love will bring us to this full restoration of relationship. First, full restoration with God and then with our brother and sister.

PRAY THIS PRAYER:

Use me, Lord, to destroy the works of satan, not only in my life but also, in the lives of others with whom I'm in contact every day. Give me the courage to speak up and correct those who gossip and lay guilt trips on others through my lifestyle, example and my words of love. Help me not to be neutral, but to be on Your side in this warfare that is all around me. Deliver me from the fear of people and instill in me the fear of the Lord Amen.

STUDY QUESTIONS

1. Of the seven steps to complete forgiveness we just covered, which one do you think will be the hardest for you? Why?

2. Based on what you have learned throughout this book, what can you do to take this most difficult step?

3. Meditate on Matt. 5:44. Write it out 3 times and commit it to memory.

CHAPTER TWELVE
WALKING IN THE TRUTH

We have certainly covered a lot of ground in this book. But now it is important to practice these steps until they become a way of life—until we operate every day in a lifestyle of forgiveness. We believe that the Spirit of the Lord has taught us how to walk the journey as an extension of His presence and an exhibition of His power. **As we continue to walk in this forgiveness, we will see that our body will be healthier, our outlook will be brighter and more hopeful and our relationships will be restored.** Many people are weak, frail and subject to all kinds of diseases because of unforgiveness. By understanding the principles in this book and applying them I believe that many of us will receive freedom as evil powers over our lives are broken and we are set free from the devastation of unforgiveness, from bloodlines, and transference of spirits in the mother's womb. I believe that we will find a new freedom to worship God and love others like never before, because there's now a new Holy Spirit boldness inside. God will help us forgive those who hurt us, whether recently or from many years ago.

Now that we have been set free, we need to take measures to guard ourselves. We must be serious worshippers of God. Our minds and hearts need to be protected so we do not go back into old habit patterns. A little leaven will spoil the whole lump. It does not take much to pull us back. It is easy to get back into old habit patterns. They fit us so well, like a comfortable old coat. **We are like the salmon fighting its way upstream every day, struggling against our human nature—that sinful part of us that tries to overtake us.** Let's protect ourselves and make a decision today to be an extension of God's presence and the exhibition of His power. From this day forward, let's be people who walk in the ministry of reconciliation, Christ's ambassadors carrying our cross daily. When the flesh gives you a hard time, crucify it!

Satan will test and try your faith. That is why James 1:2 says to count it all joy when you fall into many trials and temptations. There will be tests every day on this subject and it's completely up to you whether or not you pass. As you pass, you will graduate to the next level. You have just completed Forgiveness 101 and God is going to promote you, but before you graduate you are going to take a test. The test may be a person standing in your face and cursing you. I don't know exactly what form your test will take, but it *will* come.

Somebody will come against you and make things hard for you. Someone will do the unthinkable and you will have to ask yourself: "Did I really get this forgiveness thing rooted in my heart? Am I willing to submit to the will of God?" **This forgiveness message is for everyone, but not everybody will receive and obey it. Determine to be one of those courageous few who does.** I believe there is a remnant who are willing to walk the walk and talk the talk, a remnant that is willing to take this great step of faith for the rest of their lives and no longer be tossed by every wind of doctrine. Are you among them? Are you part of that remnant God is looking for?

Do you want to get into the full time ministry of reconciliation that God has ordained you to? Or do you want to stay where you are, let life pass you by and miss your call here on this earth? I believe that today God is going to empower you to walk as Christ's ambassador in this ministry of reconciliation, so you can be used by Him in a mighty way to restore those who are outside of fellowship with Him. By knowing and understanding all about forgiveness, we can know and understand God. It says in Daniel 11:32b:

> ....but the people who know their God shall be strong, and carry out great exploits. (Daniel 11:32b, NKJV)

Will you answer the call of God to bring you into places where you can walk in God's divine favor and release divine forgiveness and love to those who are around you? Accept the mantle of the ministry of reconciliation today. Put on the full armor of God and be strong in the power of His might. Do not back down. You know what your call is.

By taking this stand today, healing and restoration is going to be released in your relationships. God will equip you with supernatural power. People are going to look into your eyes and find Jesus. They might be angry at you, but when they look into your eyes, through the window of your soul, they will see the power of God; and their hearts are going to melt. Because of the love of God they see flowing through you despite your circumstances, they are going to come to the saving knowledge of Jesus.

Will it be painful at times? Yes, it will be upsetting and difficult at times.

For our light affliction, which is but for a moment, worketh for us a far more exceeding and eternal weight of glory. (II Corinthians 4:17)

If you truly want to experience God's glory, then say yes to the discomfort, the "light affliction". You will go through, you will break through and you will release the glory of God! The miracle power of God will more than make up for any suffering you endure. God will make sure that your destiny will be fulfilled because He is looking for ambassadors for Christ.

Before you close this book and put it on the shelf, I would like you to seal the things that God has shown you in prayer. We know that the enemy comes immediately to steal the Word, especially a word about forgiveness! This subject is very important, so I would like you to take a moment and pray the prayer below. But you need to mean it from your heart. Do not make a vow rashly. May the peace of God guard and protect you as you walk out your healing. God bless you!

PRAY THIS PRAYER:

In the name of Jesus, help me to be Christ's ambassador. With the help of the Holy Spirit, I will go forward to be a testimony, not a "testiphony", of my Lord and Savior. I will put a walk to the talk and not be a hypocrite, but a true light to the world and salt of the earth to fulfill my call as a child of God in my family, in my marriage, in my community and on my job. I promise today to be a vessel of honor that is useful for the Master, prepared unto every good work. Whenever I am tempted to withhold forgiveness to another, remind me of Your forgiveness for me so I can forgive them as I have been forgiven. When I fall short, I will quickly repent, ask Your forgiveness and let You wash me with the blood of Jesus. I am a righteous man/woman. I may fall seven times, but You, Lord, will lift me up and place my feet on the solid Rock. I will accomplish the destiny that you have placed in my heart. I will lead many to Jesus. Many will see the love and forgiveness of Jesus in me. Lord, I will not be easily put off. I will not be agitated and turned back to the old way of living, for I am a new person in Christ. I will shake off every offense before it can take root. Today, I confirm it with this oath. I am more than a conqueror in Jesus Christ. It has been predetermined in my life that I be conformed to the image of Jesus Christ. I will reign over my circumstances through one Christ Jesus from this day forward. AMEN!

STUDY QUESTIONS

1. Take time to meditate on Isaiah 43:18 and 19 and commit it to memory.

2. How do you think you will handle confrontations and offense differently now that you have read this book?

3. We believe you'll see God's miracle power unfold in your life as you put these principles to work. As an ongoing project to record your progress on this journey to total healing, start a personal journal. Every day, spend time in prayer and the Word of God, writing down what you receive. Also, be sure to record the victories in your relationships!

ABOUT THE AUTHORS

Gaspar Anastasi is Bishop of Word Of Life Ministries which consists of sixteen churches worldwide. In 2003, the headquarters for Word Of Life Ministries was relocated from Freeport, New York to Fort Myers, Florida, where Bishop Gaspar & Michele now pastor Word Of Life Church.

Sensing a strong apostolic call on his life, in 1997, Bishop Anastasi founded Global Leaders Fellowship International (formerly Global Church Fellowship) for which he serves as Executive Director. GLFI is a fellowship of churches whose purpose is to train, encourage and support church leaders worldwide while imparting a heart for Israel and the Jewish people.

In 1985, the Anastasi's founded Word Of Life Ministries Bible Education Center to help train up the Body of Christ as God's mighty army; and, in 1983, founded the New Life Centers, a rehabilitation program for drug and alcohol abusers. The New Life Centers recently celebrated their 20th anniversary and today, with the help of Jesus Christ, have delivered hundreds of men and women from the bondage of drug and alcohol addiction and other dysfunctional lifestyles.

In more than 25 years of ministry and through the leading of the Holy Spirit, the Anastasi's have developed a focus for total healing—spirit, soul, body and relationships. As a result of Word Of Life's unique and effective prayer counseling ministry, many people have been healed of deep emotional scars caused by past hurts and rejection and now live lives that are whole and productive. Together they have also pioneered a highly successful marriage counseling ministry and conduct Marriage Conferences as well as conferences on Spiritual Warfare, Damaged Emotions & Past Hurts, Leadership Development and the Church & Israel.

Pastor Michele leads Word Of Life's own Women Caring for Women ministry and is active in women's leadership development. They also air a weekly television program "God Has the Answer" in the Southwest Florida area, and he has written close to a dozen books. They have been married 40 years and have five children and four grandchildren.

Books by Bishop Gaspar Anastasi

Why Storms Are Good For Your Life

Seven Steps to Complete Forgiveness

God's Answer to Depression

A Light Unto My Path: Daily Meditations

How to Grow a Church God's Way

Countdown to Your Breakthrough

Third Day Evangelism

This is War

Discerning the Right Decision

How to be a Lion Hunter

Freedom from Anger

Stop Hurting Start Healing

If you would like to receive one or more of these publications, please write to: Word Of Life Church, 2150 Collier Ave., Suite H, Fort Myers, Florida 33901 or call (239) 274-8881. You may also order books as well as teaching tapes and CD's from our website: www.WOLM.net

BOOKS & BOOKLETS

BY BISHOP GASPAR ANASTASI

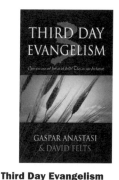

This is War The forces of hell have declared war on the Church. The question is: Will the Army of the Living God rise to the occasion? 144pp

Countdown to Your Breakthrough From time to time, we all get discouraged. This book will help you develop a strategy to demolish strongholds and get in line with God's plan for your life. 80pp

Third Day Evangelism This is the era Hosea called the Third Day when God's glory will cover the earth. Learn to impact your neighborhood—and eternity—for Christ! 144pp

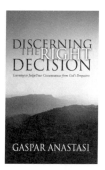

Discerning the Right Decision Bishop Anastasi shows you how to make choices that will bless you and lead you into the abundant life Jesus came to give. 60pp

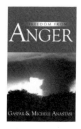

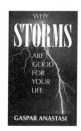

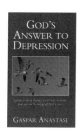

BOOKLETS: *Freedom from Anger • Why Storms Are Good for Your Life Seven Steps to Complete Forgiveness • God's Answer to Depression*

Call **(239) 274-8881** or order through our website **www.WOLM.net**

WORD OF LIFE MINISTRIES
PRAYER COUNSELING SERIES
BY BISHOP GASPAR & MICHELE ANASTASI

These are intensive Bible Studies taken directly from the highly successful Prayer Counseling Ministry pioneered by Bishop Gaspar & Michele Anastasi. They combine a thorough study of the Word of God through Teaching Tapes, Meditation Booklet and other materials with a personal time of prayer and praise. They are sure to be a blessing to you—spirit, soul, body and relationships.

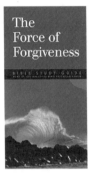
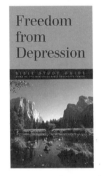
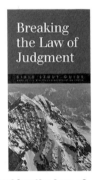

The Force of Forgiveness
Includes 8 Teaching Tapes, Meditation Booklet & *Seven Steps to Complete Forgiveness* Booklet.

Freedom from Depression
Includes 7 Teaching Tapes, Meditation Booklet, *God's Answer to Depression* Booklet, & "Who I Am in Christ" Confession Sheet.

Breaking the Law of Judgment Includes 4 Teaching Tapes, Meditation Booklet & *Seven Steps to Complete Forgiveness* Booklet.

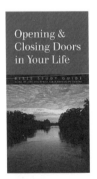

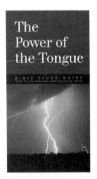

Opening & Closing Doors in Your Life Includes 6 Teaching Tapes & Meditation Booklet.

Overcoming Temporary Defeat Includes 8 Teaching Tapes & Meditation Booklet.

The Power of the Tongue
Includes 8 Teaching Tapes, Meditation Booklet & "Who I Am in Christ" Confession Sheet.

Call **(239) 274-8881** or order through our website **www.WOLM.net**